11th Workshop on Patent and Scientific Literature Translation (PSLT 2025)

Geneva, Switzerland
24 June 2025

ISBN: 979-8-3313-2673-9

Printed from e-media with permission by:

Curran Associates, Inc.
57 Morehouse Lane
Red Hook, NY 12571

Some format issues inherent in the e-media version may also appear in this print version.

Association for Computational Linguistics
209 N. Eighth Street
Stroudsburg, Pennsylvania 18360

Phone: 1-570-476-8006
Fax: 1-570-476-0860

acl@aclweb.org

Additional copies of this publication are available from:

Curran Associates, Inc.
57 Morehouse Lane
Red Hook, NY 12571 USA
Phone: 845-758-0400
Fax: 845-758-2633
Email: curran@proceedings.com
Web: www.proceedings.com

pslt 2025

11th Workshop on Patent and Scientific Literature Translation (PSLT 2025)

Proceedings of the Workshop

June 24, 2025

Geneva, Switzerland

Message from the Organising Committee

The workshop on Patent and Scientific Literature Translation (PSLT) focuses on the translation of patent documents and any kind of technical and scientific literature. This workshop series began in 2005 at the tenth Machine Translation Summit, and we are delighted to have the eleventh edition of the workshop in Geneva, Switzerland at the twentieth Machine Translation Summit.

Machine translation technologies have advanced drastically in this decade through deep learning techniques. We are now at a turning point from Neural Machine Translation with the encoder-decoder framework to Large Language Model-based Translation with the decoder-only architecture. This transition is not limited to translation; we can use Large Language Models to assist writing and to proofread technical and scientific literature. In the PSLT workshop this year, we will discuss our future of the translation of technical and scientific documents and the multilingual dissemination of novel technical achievements and scientific findings beyond the language barrier.

This workshop features two keynote talks by Ryota Murakami (Japan Patent Office; JPO) and Bruno Pouliquen (World Intellectual Property Organization; WIPO). Mr. Murakami will present JPO's activities for their patent information platform. Mr. Pouliquen will present WIPO Translate and their activities in the intellectual property field. The workshop also accepted two technical papers about scientific literature translation. We hope we can share ideas and insights related to the focus of this workshop.

We express our sincere appreciation to the keynote speakers and the paper authors as well as the program committee members and the organizing committee members of the MT Summit 2025. We also appreciate the help of AAMT/Japio Special Interest Group on Patent Translation for organizing this workshop.

Katsuhito Sudoh
Takashi Tsunakawa
Isao Goto

Organising Committee

Takashi Tsunakawa	Shizuoka University, Japan
Katsuhito Sudoh	Nara Women's University, Japan
Isao Goto	Ehime University, Japan

Programme Committee

Hailong Cao	Harbin Institute of Technology
Chenhui Chu	Kyoto University
Toshiaki Nakazawa	The University of Tokyo
Takashi Ninomiya	Ehime University
Naoaki Okazaki	Institute of Science Tokyo
Akihiro Tamura	Doshisha University
Yuki Arase	Institute of Science Tokyo
Hiroshi Echizen'ya	Hokkai-Gakuen University
Kenji Imamura	National Institute of Information and Communications Technology (NICT)
Genichiro Kikui	Japan Science and Technology Agency
Mamoru Komachi	Hitotsubashi University
Sadao Kurohashi	National Institute of Informatics
Satoshi Sonoh	Toshiba Digital Solutions Corporation
Jun Suzuki	Tohoku University
Jun'ichi Tsujii	National Institute of Advanced Industrial Science and Technology (AIST)
Xiangli Wang	Deep Language Co.,Ltd.
Taro Watanabe	Nara Institute of Science and Technology (NAIST)

Keynote Talk
Initiatives Related to Machine Translation at the Japan Patent Office

Ryota Murakami
Japan Patent Office

Abstract: The Japan Patent Office (JPO) provides IT services to users for accessing patent information, and through the J-PlatPat platform, English machine translation is offered, which is publicly accessible to both domestic and international users. Recently, J-PlatPat has been updated to improve functionality for users, enhancing various features. Additionally, the JPO is creating bilingual dictionaries and parallel corpora for higher-priority languages to expand machine translation capabilities. They are also conducting research on the effectiveness of improving translation quality through training the machine translation engine, and the research reports are publicly available. In this presentation, he will discuss the updates to J-PlatPat, report on the results of the research project related to machine translation, and outline the initiatives regarding machine translation of patent information at the JPO.

Keynote Talk

Advancing Patent and Scientific Literature Translation: WIPO Translate and other tools available at WIPO

Bruno Pouilquen
World Intellectual Property Organization

Abstract: In this presentation, Mr. Bruno Pouliquen from the World Intellectual Property Organization (WIPO) will discuss the advancements in patent and scientific literature translation, with a focus on WIPO's in-house tool: WIPO Translate. This is specifically trained for patents and is fully integrated in WIPO search engine Patentscope, it currently covers 17 languages and is also used for non-patent literature (NPL) translation. The presentation will delve into the development and application of WIPO Translate, highlighting its role in improving accessibility and understanding of intellectual property across linguistic barriers. In addition, Mr. Pouliquen will present automatic classification using the International Patent Classification (IPC) system, also used to classify NPL documents. He will also share insights on WIPO's experiments with image similarity, speech-processing and Large Language Models (LLMs) in the intellectual property field.

Table of Contents

GenAIese - A Comprehensive Comparison of GPT-4o and DeepSeek-V3 for English-to-Chinese Academic Translation

Longhui Zou[1], Ke Li [2], Joshua Lamerton[3], Mehdi Mirzapour[3]

[1]University of Montana, [2]Guangdong University of Foreign Studies, [3]PropTexx USA

Correspondence: lzou4@kent.edu

Abstract

This study investigates the translation performance of two recent large language models—ChatGPT-4o and DeepSeek-V3—in translating English academic papers on language, culture, and literature into Chinese at the discourse level. Using a corpus of 11 academic texts totaling 3,498 sentences, we evaluated translation quality through reference-free automatic metrics (COMET-KIWI), lexical diversity indicators, and syntactic complexity measures. Our findings reveal an interesting contrast: while DeepSeek-V3 achieves higher overall quality scores, GPT-4o produces translations with consistently greater lexical richness (higher type-token ratio, standardized TTR, average sentence length, and word entropy) and syntactic complexity across all five measured metrics, such as Incomplete Dependency Theory Metric (IDT), Dependency Locality Theory Metric (DLT), Combined IDT+DLT Metric (IDT+DLT), Left-Embeddedness (LE), and Nested Nouns Distance (NND). Particularly notable are GPT-4o's higher scores in Left-Embeddedness and Nested Nouns Distance metrics, which are specifically relevant to Chinese linguistic patterns. The divergence between automatic quality estimation and linguistic complexity metrics highlights the multifaceted nature of machine translation quality assessment.

1 Introduction

Quality estimation (QE) of machine translation (MT) products has long been a key area of interest to both MT developers and translation scholars. A wide range of QE methods have been developed to provide information on improving and selecting MT systems. At the same time, specific features in machine-involved translation products, such as high levels of semantic and syntactic literality and unidiomatic target language expressions, have also attracted great research interest, offering implications for further understanding of MT systems and the design of more reliable and valid QE methods. For statistical and neural machine translation (NMT) systems, MT outputs tend to be easily influenced by source text structure, exhibiting a stronger structural shining-through effect, lower level of target-text normalization and reduced linguistic richness when compared to from-scratch human translation products (Bizzoni et al., 2020; Vanmassenhove et al., 2021). Those features, referred to as "machine translationese", will further bring an effect on downstream post-editors, leading to "post-editese" – features distinguishing post-editing products from from-scratch translation products, including lexical simplification and more salient syntactic influence from the source text (Toral, 2019).

The performance of large language models (LLMs) applied to translation tasks has been proven promising. LLMs outperformed commercial NMT models in various language pairs when it comes to document-level translation (Kocmi et al., 2024; Wang et al., 2023). Wang et al. (2023) found that the strength of GPT-powered translation is more salient when it comes to human evaluation, possibly due to its advantage in contextual coherence and naturalness of the target language. The better ability of context awareness in GPT-powered translation over NMT systems is proved by Castilho et al. (2023), who found the advantage in all tested language pairs except a low-resource pair (English-Irish). LLM-powered translation is also found to be less literal compared to NMT systems when translating out of English (Raunak et al., 2023), showing its potential in tackling issues of machine translationese. However, a comparison of translation error types between ChatGPT and NMT systems found more frequent over-translation and mistranslation

Proceedings of the Eleventh Workshop on Patent and Scientific Literature Translation (PSLT 2025), pages 1–12, June 24, 2025

errors in GPT-powered translation, suggesting the problem of hallucinations in LLM-powered translation (Jiao et al., 2023).

Despite the research effort in investigating LLM-powered translations, previous studies mostly followed quality assessment methods used in assessing MT outputs, either on a sentence level or on a document level of a short length. Such a short evaluation unit might prevent us from exploring linguistic issues that will probably bring negative effects to the users in real-life translation settings, for example, cohesion and coherence issues. This concern is particularly significant in the translation of academic papers, as these texts are typically lengthy, feature complex syntactic structures, and demand high accuracy in terminology. Rendering academic papers on topics such as language, culture and literature is even more challenging. These papers are often rich in cultural-loaded expressions, wordplays, and quotations of literary works, making them complex combinations of technical and creative texts. Therefore, translating such papers requires a high level of accuracy and creativity.

Previous research highlights that translators often face challenges in maintaining consistency, choosing precise terminology, and adapting to evolving technical language (Al-Smadi, 2022). Moreover, the complexity of subject matter and the need for adherence to proper academic style make the translation process time-consuming and meticulous (Paperpal, 2023). Ensuring high-quality translations requires not only linguistic proficiency but also careful proofreading and a deep understanding of the field's specialized knowledge. If LLMs can be effectively tested and proven capable of handling these challenges, they could significantly assist professional translators and streamline the translation process by improving consistency, reducing repetitive manual corrections, and assisting with complex syntactic structures.

Therefore, there is a pressing need to explore both LLM-powered MT capabilities and corresponding QE methods at the discourse level. This dual focus would not only advance the development of more sophisticated translation technologies but also ensure reliable quality assessment methods that can effectively evaluate long-form translations, considering factors such as terminology consistency, cross-reference accuracy, and overall document coherence.

The present paper reports a study on the performance of LLM-powered MT products under the context of academic translation. Our focus is on comparing the performance of two non-reasoning models, namely, ChatGPT-4o and Deepseek-V3, in English-Chinese translation. Deepseek-V3 is a free-access model recently released in December 2024. Although user feedback on the use of Deekseek in translation tasks is generally positive, experts in the language industry remain skeptical of its translation capability, pointing out that it did not outperform other mainstream LLMs in some language pairs and domain-specific use cases (Slator, 2024). This calls for a systematic evaluation of Deepseek-powered translation products before reaching a solid conclusion on its translation performance. The significance of this study lies in its examination of Deepseek's translation capabilities since its recent launch. The investigation comes at a critical moment in the way that machine translation increasingly handles complex document-level tasks. This research addresses two notable gaps in the current literature: First, it provides early empirical evidence of Deepseek's translation performance, contributing to our understanding of emerging large language models; second, it offers a systematic comparison with ChatGPT at the discourse level, moving beyond the more common sentence-level evaluations. This comprehensive analysis at the discourse level is particularly valuable as it better reflects real-world translation scenarios and reveals how these models handle broader context and maintain consistency across longer texts.

2 Methodology

11 English open-access research papers published in linguistic journals were selected as source texts (STs) in this study. To facilitate the evaluation process and ensure consistent comparison across models, their titles, sub-titles, tables, figures, notes, bibliography, acknowledgments, and appendices were removed. This preprocessing step was necessary to focus our analysis on the continuous prose sections that form the core content of academic papers, eliminating structural elements that might be handled differently by LLM systems and potentially skewing the comparative results.

The STs totaled 3,498 sentences (93,865 tokens), covering a range of topics including language, culture, and literature. Examples appeared in some articles that involve languages other than English (1,044 tokens) were removed when calculating readability indices. Profiling of the STs is reported in Table 1, in which the Flesch Reading Ease score (RDFRE), the Flesch-Kincaid Grade Level (RDFKGL), and the Coh-Metrix L2 Readability (RDL2), as indicators of text complexity, were calculated by the Coh-Metrix software (McNamara et al., 2014). Flesch Reading Ease score (RDFRE) measures the readability of a text based primarily on sentence length and word length (syllable count). Lower RDFRE scores indicate more complex text, while higher scores indicate more easy-to-read text. In our data, ST1 has the lowest RDFRE (18.206) and is described as the most complex.

Flesch-Kincaid Grade Level (RDFKGL) estimates the US school grade level required to understand the text. Higher scores indicate that more advanced education is needed to comprehend the text. For example, a score of 12 suggests a high school senior level, while 16+ suggests college graduate level. In our data, ST9 has the highest RDFKGL (18.157), suggesting it requires post-graduate level education to comprehend.

Coh-Metrix L2 Readability (RDL2) is specifically designed to assess text difficulty for second language learners. It incorporates additional linguistic features beyond sentence and word length, including cohesion, syntactic complexity, and lexical diversity. Lower RDL2 scores indicate text that would be more challenging for non-native speakers. In our dataset, ST11 has the lowest RDL2 (7.161), suggesting it would be particularly difficult for second language readers.

Overall, the readability scores indicate that the STs generally fall within the reading proficiency of college to graduate students who are native English speakers and are relatively difficult to comprehend by L2 English speakers (Flesch, 1979).

The STs were translated by ChatGPT-4o and Deepseek-V3 with the same prompt: "You are a professional translator working with academic texts. Translate this from English to Chinese: ST". We chose the models for two reasons. First, they are likely to be accepted by users in need of English-Chinese machine translation. In a recent survey among Chinese professional translators, 75.5% respondents reported use of ChatGPT as translation aid (Shi et al., 2024). Deepseek-V3 is reported to achieve "performance comparable to leading closed-source models, including ChatGPT-4o and Claude-3.5-Sonnet, on a series of standard and open-ended benchmark" and "surpasses these models in Chinese factual knowledge" (Liu et al., 2024), showing its potential in conducting English-to-Chinese translation tasks.

Second, they can generate the entire target text more effectively than newer reasoning models. In our pilot study, we tested the state-of-the-art reasoning model Deepseek-R1, released on January 20th. We observed that the R1 model tended to omit parts of sentences or entire sentences to a large extent in its translations. As shown in Table 2, with the same set of STs, the total target tokens generated by DeepSeek-R1 amount to only 59.87% of the mean total target tokens generated by ChatGPT-4o and DeepSeek-V3. The inclination of reasoning-capable language models to omit sentences and introduce creative elements during translation may arise from a fundamental tension between their reasoning abilities and the need for translation fidelity. As explored by He et al. (2024) in their study on human-like translation strategies, these models can emulate human translators by analyzing the ST and generating background knowledge to guide the translation process. This approach can lead to what He et al. (2024) describe as "creative reformulation," where the model restructures content based Liu et al. (2023) indicates that models with strong reasoning capabilities may produce "logical completions" during translation, potentially diverging from the original text in favor of outputs that the model deems more contextually appropriate or logically coherent. We plan to compare the translation performance of DeepSeek-R1 with OpenAI's recently released ChatGPT-4.5 model, which was introduced on February 27, 2025 (OpenAI, 2025). In this study, the responses of DeepSeek-R1 and DeepSeek-V3 were generated from its official website [1].

3 Automatic Quality Estimation

In this paper, we use COMET-KIWI [2] as the automatic tool for QE, as it provides a more comprehensive and linguistically informed evaluation of MT outputs. Unlike BLEU(Papineni et al., 2002), which primarily measures lexical and syntactic similarity based on n-gram overlaps, COMET-KIWI captures deeper semantic relationships between the source and translation. This ability allows it to assess meaning more effectively, making it robust to variations in word choice and paraphrasing that

[1] https://chat.deepseek.com/

[2] https://huggingface.co/Unbabel/wmt22-cometkiwi-da

ST index	Topics	RDFRE	RDFKGL	RDL2
ST1	Sociolinguistic scales	18.206	17.774	8.086
ST2	Food translation	35.401	14.666	11.857
ST3	Thought-language identification	33.758	14.407	12.575
ST4	Deceptive communication	38.201	14.584	10.488
ST5	Neurophenomenal space	39.854	12.810	9.662
ST6	Language-thought dependency	33.222	16.249	14.120
ST7	Pictorial assertion	48.425	12.644	17.876
ST8	Translation cognition	34.419	14.422	9.437
ST9	Translanguaging	23.568	18.157	10.062
ST10	Multilingualism & ethics	30.860	15.624	9.932
ST11	Poetic Technicity	37.566	13.524	7.161
Average		33.950	14.990	11.020

Table 1: Profiling of Source Texts

ST index	ST Segment count	ST Tokens	TT Tokens_DS R1	TT Tokens_DS V3	TT Tokens_GPT-4o
ST1	70	2049	1668	1911	2057
ST2	271	7936	4034	6961	7490
ST3	650	15814	7220	13966	15620
ST4	310	8709	5401	8376	9102
ST5	347	7383	4856	6655	7048
ST6	199	6424	3961	5932	6167
ST7	418	10457	5908	9174	9521
ST8	345	8862	4976	8097	8423
ST9	317	10998	4762	10048	10511
ST10	308	8447	5148	7486	7492
ST11	263	6786	4038	5386	6191
Total	3498	93865	51972	83992	89622

Table 2: Word Counts for different LLM models

traditional metrics often fail to recognize. Additionally, COMET-KIWI can function as a reference-free QE model, meaning it does not require a high-quality reference translation for comparison. This is particularly valuable in real-world applications and low-resource language settings where reference translations may not always be available. Research has shown that COMET-based models, including COMET-KIWI, correlate more strongly with human evaluations than BLEU and other traditional metrics such as TER and METEOR(Rei et al., 2022; Agarwal and Lavie, 2008). BLEU often fails to capture fluency and adequacy effectively, especially in cases where an NMT system produces highly fluent yet paraphrased translations. In contrast, COMET-KIWI's deep learning-based approach aligns more closely with how humans assess translation quality, making it a more reliable metric.

According to the results of overall COMET scores at text level, DeepSeek-V3 (DS-V3) demonstrates superior performance overall with an average COMET score of 0.7790, compared to ChatGPT-4o (GPT-4o)'s 0.7655. This 0.0135 point advantage, while seemingly modest, is consistent across nearly all texts (10 out of 11) and suggests a meaningful difference in translation quality.

As shown in Figure 1, DS-V3 shows more consistent performance across different STs. Its scores range from 0.6847 to 0.8171, whereas GPT-4o shows greater variability, with scores ranging from 0.6514 to 0.8074. This suggests DS-V3 may offer more reliable quality across diverse topics or text complexity levels.

The relationship between text complexity (readability) metrics and translation performance of the LLMs demonstrates inconsistent patterns. As illustrated in Table 3, the weak to moderate correlations between readability metrics and COMET scores suggest that traditional measures of text difficulty for human readers do not directly translate to difficulty for LLM-powered MT. The correlation between RDFRE and DS-V3 translation performance ($r = -0.31$, $p > 0.05$) suggests a moderate negative relationship, though not statistically significant given our relatively small sample size. For GPT-4o, this correlation is even weaker ($r = -0.14$, $p > 0.05$), suggesting its performance may be influenced by different factors altogether. Similarly, the correlations between performance and other readability metrics (RDFKGL: $r = 0.25$ for DS-V3, $r = 0.17$ for GPT-4o; RDL2: $r = 0.11$ for DS-V3, $r = 0.04$ for GPT-4o) fail to reach statistical significance, further suggesting that these models may be less sensitive to surface linguistic features and more influenced by content complexity and contextual factors.

The most revealing insights emerge from examining specific STs. ST3 (Thought-language identification) exhibits the largest performance gap (0.1292) between DS-V3 and GPT-4o despite having only moderate complexity scores (RDFRE: 33.76, RDFKGL: 14.41, RDL2: 12.58). GPT-4o's dramatic underperformance on this specialized linguistic content indicates a significant weakness in handling certain conceptual ambiguity.

Conversely, ST1 (Sociolinguistic scales), the formally most complex text (lowest RDFRE: 18.206, second lowest RDL2: 8.086), shows strong and nearly identical performance from both models (DS-V3: 0.8171, GPT-4o: 0.8041). A likely explanation is that ST1's content domain may contain terminology and concepts that are well-represented in the training data of both models. Even though the text is structurally complex, the semantic content may be more accessible to these models compared to other domains. Alternatively, the text may be complex but internally consistent in its terminology and logical reasoning patterns, making it more manageable for the LLMs to translate despite its high readability scores.

The correlation between performance gap and readability measures is minimal (RDFRE: $r = -0.11$; RDFKGL: $r = 0.005$; RDL2: $r = 0.05$; all $p > 0.05$), reinforcing that domain-specific knowledge rather than general readability differentiates these models' translation performance. While COMET-KIWI and similar QE metrics provide a general assessment of MT quality of both LLMs, their performance in terms of lexical diversity and syntactic complexity is worth further investigation as part of their translation quality evaluation (Yu, 2024).

4 Comparison of Lexical diversity between DS-V3 and GPT-4o

Lexical diversity refers to the variety and richness of vocabulary used in a text, representing a crucial factor in assessing translation quality (Kim, 2020). It is typically measured through metrics such as type-token ratio (TTR), moving-average TTR (MATTR), and measure of textual lexical diversity (MTLD) (McCarthy, 2005; Koizumi, 2012). Previous studies have indicated that MT systems

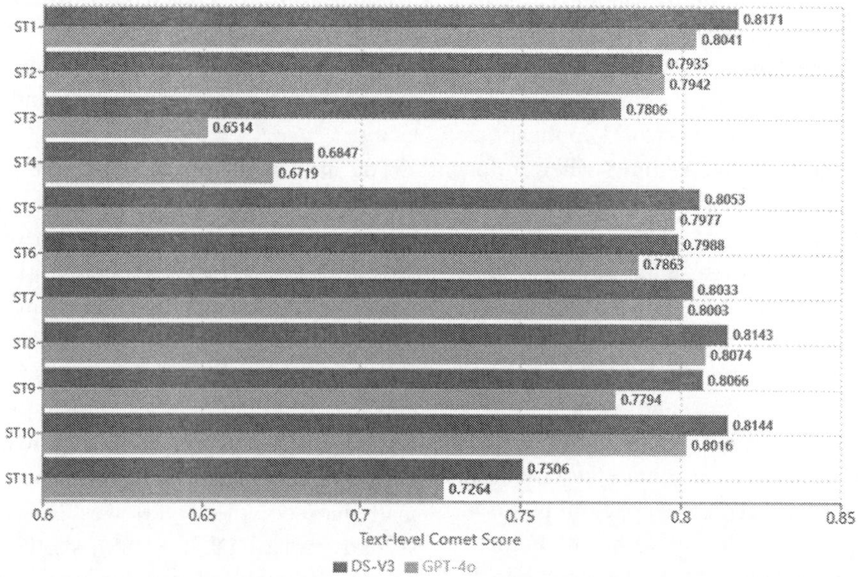

Figure 1: Comparison of Text-level Comet Score between DeepSeek-V3 (DS-V3) and ChatGPT-4o (GPT-4o)

Readability Metric	DS-V3 Score	GPT-4o Score	Performance Gap
RDFRE	-0.31 ($p > 0.05$)	-0.14 ($p > 0.05$)	-0.11 ($p > 0.05$)
RDFKGL	0.25 ($p > 0.05$)	0.17 ($p > 0.05$)	0.01 ($p > 0.05$)
RDL2	0.11 ($p > 0.05$)	0.04 ($p > 0.05$)	0.05 ($p > 0.05$)

Table 3: Correlation Between Readability Metrics and LLM Translation Quality

often produce outputs with lower lexical diversity compared to human translations, exhibiting tendencies toward vocabulary simplification and repetition(Fu and Nederhof, 2021). This phenomenon is partly due to MT systems favoring the most probable translations based on their training data, which can lead to the reduction of alternative expressions and a conformity to well-documented modes of expression. These patterns have been documented across various language pairs and domains, with earlier NMT systems particularly struggling to maintain lexical richness when translating stylistically complex texts (Brglez and Vintar, 2022).

While advancements in LLMs promise improved translation quality, their ability to maintain lexical diversity remains an area of active investigation. In this paper, we compare the lexical diversity of translation outputs produced by GPT-4o and DS-V3 at discourse level using our dataset of academic papers on topics such as language, culture, and literature. The translation of such papers demands both precision and creativity, making them ideal test sets for evaluating advanced LLMs' ability to maintain lexical richness while preserving semantic accuracy.

We first calculate traditional lexical diversity metrics using the WordSmith tool to analyze surface linguistic features in the translated texts by both GPT-4o and DS-V3. These metrics include type-token ratio (TTR), which is the ratio of unique words to total words; standardized type-token ratio (STTR), which is TTR calculated per 1,000-word segments to control for text length effects; and average sentence length (ASL), measured by the word count of each target text segment corresponding to a source text sentence.

To provide a more comprehensive assessment of lexical diversity, we also incorporate word entropy (WE) as an additional indicator. While TTR and STTR measure vocabulary diversity based on the proportion of unique words relative to total words, they do not capture the randomness and unpredictability of word usage within a text. Entropy, derived from information theory (Shannon, 1948), quantifies the degree of uncertainty in word distribution, offering a more refined understanding of lexical variation in the translated text. A higher

WE value indicates greater word unpredictability and diversity, suggesting a richer and more varied vocabulary, though potentially increasing reading difficulty (Liu et al., 2022).

Our results of lexical diversity metrics, including TTR, STTR, ASL, and WE show that GPT-4o consistently outperforms DS-V3 across all four lexical diversity metrics when translating English academic papers on language, culture, and literature into Chinese. GPT-4o shows a notably higher TTR (approximately 21.80% vs 19.99% for DS-V3), which suggests its translations contain a richer vocabulary variety. The average 9.06% higher TTR indicates GPT-4o produces less repetitive translations than DS-V3 in our dataset.

In terms of STTR, GPT-4o maintains an advantage (approximately 42.24 vs 39.08 for DS-V3). The 8.08% higher STTR confirms that GPT-4o's higher lexical diversity is consistent even when controlling for text length.

For ASL, GPT-4o produces consistently longer sentences (around 26.5 words compared to 22.3 words for DS-V3). This nearly 19% difference in average sentence length aligns with our findings in Table 2, which shows that when translating the same set of STs, GPT-4o generates 89,622 target tokens, while DS-V3 produces 83,922 tokens—representing 6.79% more target tokens overall. This consistent pattern across both sentence-level and document-level measurements reinforces the observation that GPT-4o tends to create more elaborated translations.

Regarding WE, GPT-4o demonstrates slightly higher word entropy (approximately 5.85 vs 5.74 for DS-V3). The 1.78% higher WE indicates GPT-4o translations have a more balanced distribution of word frequencies, leading to a richer and more varied vocabulary. This suggests that GPT-4o tends to produce more information-rich content with less predictable word choices.

As illustrated in the radar chart of Figure 2, the differences between these two models are not uniform across all metrics. The most pronounced differences appear in ASL and TTR, while WE shows the smallest difference. This pattern not only suggests that GPT-4o employs a broader vocabulary range, but may also indicate that its translation approach preserves more complex sentence structures of the original texts than DS-V3. We will further examine this possibility through syntactic complexity metrics in the following section.

5 Comparison of syntactic complexity between translations of DS-V3 and GPT-4o

In this study, we computed five syntactic metrics for each of the 3,498 segments in our dataset, including the Incomplete Dependency Theory Metric (IDT), Dependency Locality Theory Metric (DLT), Combined IDT+DLT Metric (IDT+DLT), Left-Embeddedness (LE), and Nested Nouns Distance (NND). The IDT, DLT, and IDT+DLT metrics are based on linguistic complexity theories derived from Gibson's Incomplete Dependency Theory (IDT) and Dependency Locality Theory (DLT) (Gibson, 1998; Gibson et al., 2000). The LE metric is adapted with slight modifications from Coh-Metrix analysis (Graesser et al., 2011), while NND was introduced by Zou et al. (2021). LE and NND were selected due to their relevance in capturing syntactic differences between English and Chinese (Fang, 2020).

Unlike previous studies that utilize categorical proof nets (Moot and Retoré, 2012) for syntactic representation, these metrics adopt universal dependencies (De Marneffe et al., 2021). This framework provides a consistent approach to annotating grammar, encompassing part-of-speech tagging, morphological features, and syntactic dependencies. Additionally, Blache's reformulation of Incremental Dependency Theory (IDT) and Dependency Length Theory (DLT) (Blache, 2011a,b) is applied for analyzing dependency relations. To parse segments in our dataset, Stanford Stanza (Qi et al., 2020) is employed to generate dependency trees. The decision to use dependency tree parsing over categorical proof nets is primarily driven by the availability of high-quality, scalable parsers like Stanza, which support a wide range of languages. Furthermore, previous research has demonstrated that dependency trees yield reliable and interpretable results, reinforcing their suitability for this study.

The definition and implementation of these metrics are detailed in Zou (2024); Zou et al. (2024). Developing these metrics allows us to assess whether GPT-4o retains more syntactic complexity of the STs compared to DS-V3. Additionally, it enables us to examine whether the syntactic complexity of the STs has a greater influence on translations generated by GPT-4o versus DS-V3 in the context of English-to-Chinese academic translations of papers on language, culture, and literature.

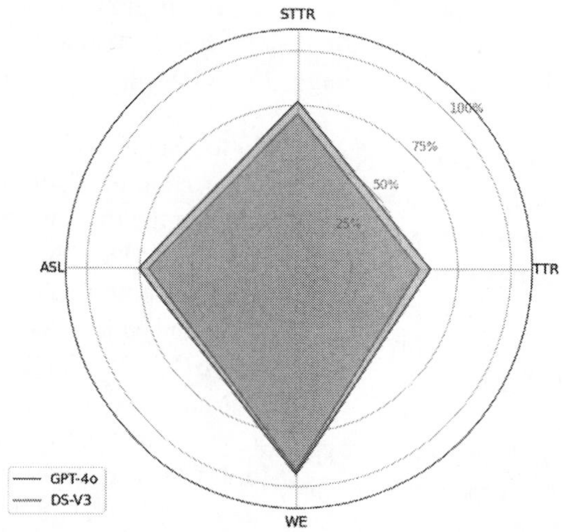

Figure 2: Comparison of Lexical Diversity Between GPT-4o and DS-V3

The results shown in Figure 3 reveal that GPT-4o consistently exhibits higher syntactic complexity than DS-V3 across all five measured metrics. These differences are statistically significant ($p < 0.05$) for all metrics, suggesting a systematic difference in the linguistic structures produced by the two models. These differences may stem from the models' underlying architectures and training data.

Incomplete Dependency Theory (IDT) counts the number of incomplete dependencies between tokens. GPT-4o shows significantly higher average IDT values (136.30) compared to DS-V3 (122.58), representing a 10.07% difference. The higher IDT values suggest that GPT-4o's outputs contain more complex syntactic structures with greater numbers of incomplete dependencies that span across the target texts. This may manifest as more sophisticated sentence constructions with multiple embedded clauses or modifying phrases.

The Dependency Locality Theory Metric (DLT) metric, which counts discourse referents (nouns, proper nouns, and verbs) between a head token and its longest leftmost dependent, is 5.28% higher in GPT-4o (13.12) compared to DS-V3 (12.43). The higher DLT values indicate GPT-4o produces target texts with longer dependency distances containing more nouns and verbs between head words and their dependents, potentially creating greater processing demands on target readers.

Not surprisingly, the combined metric shows the values of GPT-4o (149.42) are on average 9.65% higher than DS-V3 (135.01). This comprehensive measure reinforces that GPT-4o's target texts contain both more incomplete dependencies and more discourse referents within those dependencies. The significant higher values in this combined metric suggest GPT-4o's tendency toward greater overall syntactic complexity.

The Left-Embeddedness (LE) metric, which counts non-verb tokens before the main verb, shows a significant 9.89% higher value in GPT-4o (22.07) compared to DS-V3 (19.89). This difference is particularly meaningful for translations for the English-to-Chinese language pair because Chinese syntax fundamentally relies on left-embedded structures where substantial information is placed before the main verb. Topicalization in Chinese requires placing important contextual elements at the beginning of sentences, and temporal, locative, and adverbial information naturally precedes the predicate. GPT-4o's significantly higher LE score might indicate it better captures this essential characteristic of Chinese syntax, producing target text that follows the natural information flow patterns expected by the audience of native Chinese speakers.

The Nested Nouns Distance (NND) metric shows the largest percentage difference (13.20%) between the two models, with GPT-4o scoring 3.54 compared to DS-V3's 3.08. This metric is particularly relevant for English-to-Chinese translation because Chinese noun phrases follow different structural patterns than English, with modifiers strictly preceding the head noun. Chinese permits complex nested nominal structures with multiple embedded modifiers, and the distance relationships between

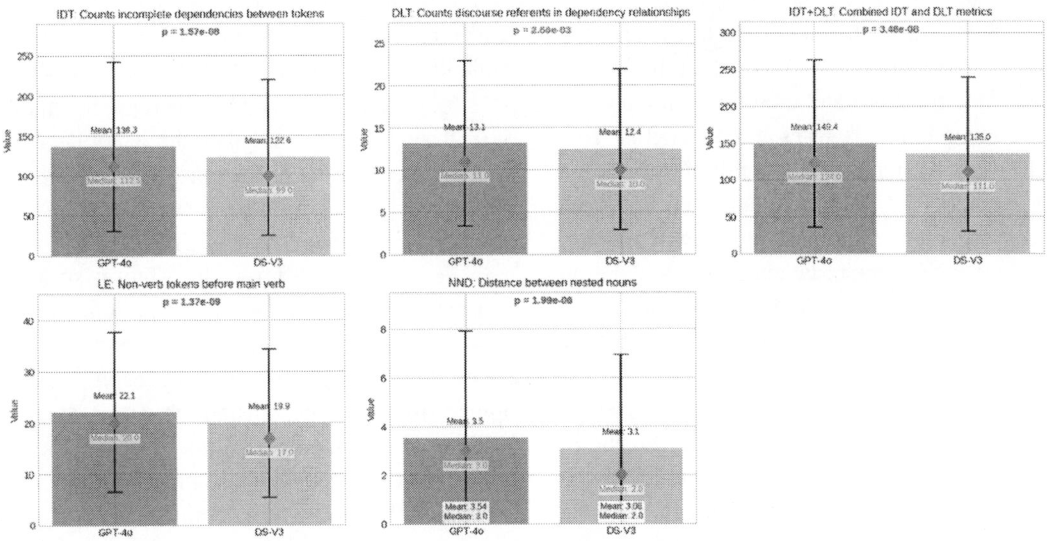

Figure 3: Comparison of Syntactic Cmplexity metrics Between Two Models

nested nouns follow language-specific conventions. GPT-4o's significantly higher NND suggests that it might better replicates the characteristic distances and relationships between nested nominal elements in Chinese. This may contribute to more authentic-sounding modifier structures and more natural nominal phrases that align with native Chinese linguistic expectations.

6 Discussion and Conclusion

This study has examined the performance of ChatGPT-4o and DeepSeek-V3 in translating English academic papers on language, literature, and culture to Chinese at the discourse level. Our analysis reveals that DeepSeek-V3 demonstrates better overall translation quality than ChatGPT-4o according to automatic quality estimation results from COMET-KIWI. DeepSeek-V3 achieved a higher average score (0.7790 versus 0.7655) and showed more consistent performance across different source texts, suggesting it may offer more reliable quality across diverse topics and complexity levels.

Interestingly, despite its lower COMET-KIWI scores, GPT-4o exhibits greater lexical richness according to all four indicators we measured. GPT-4o consistently produced translations with higher type-token ratio (21.80% versus 19.99%), standardized type-token ratio (42.24 versus 39.08), average sentence length (26.5 versus 22.3 words), and word entropy (5.85 versus 5.74). This suggests GPT-4o translations contain a more varied vocabulary and less repetitive language patterns than DeepSeek-V3.

We also found that GPT-4o's translations have greater syntactic complexity across all five segment-level metrics we examined. The higher values in Incomplete Dependency Theory (IDT), Dependency Locality Theory (DLT), combined IDT+DLT, Left-Embeddedness (LE), and Nested Nouns Distance (NND) metrics indicate GPT-4o produces more complex syntactic structures. Particularly notable are the higher scores in LE and NND, which were specifically selected as English-Chinese pair-specific metrics.

The higher syntactic complexity in LE and NND metrics might correspond to more authentic Chinese patterns, but could alternatively reflect unnecessarily complicated structures that native speakers would find awkward or unnatural. Whether this increased complexity actually results in more natural-sounding Chinese would require human evaluation by native speakers of simplified Chinese, as syntactic complexity metrics alone cannot definitively determine naturalness or fluency in the target language.

Our findings contribute to the growing body of research on what we term "GenAIese" - the distinctive linguistic characteristics of text generated by large language models. Just as previous research identified "translationese" in statistical and neural MT outputs, our study suggests that different LLM architectures may produce systematically different translation patterns that could potentially be identified using the metrics we have developed.

The divergent performance patterns between DeepSeek-V3 and GPT-4o reveal that distinct architectural foundations and training methodologies produce complementary translation strengths. This finding suggests significant opportunities for developing specialized LLM translation agents tailored to specific academic domains and communication goals. Rather than pursuing a universal translation approach, future systems could strategically leverage different architectural choices to optimize for domain-appropriate quality dimensions, whether terminological precision, syntactic naturalness, or stylistic richness. Such purpose-built translation agents could allow researchers and publishers to select models that align with disciplinary conventions, potentially transforming academic translation workflows by offering configurable balance between content fidelity and linguistic sophistication based on contextual requirements.

While our study focused on English-to-Chinese academic translation, the evaluation framework combining automatic quality assessment with lexical and syntactic complexity metrics provides a methodological foundation that can be applied to evaluate other language pairs, domains and systems. This multidimensional assessment approach addresses the limitations of relying solely on automatic metrics like COMET, which may not fully capture the linguistic qualities that contribute to translation effectiveness in specialized contexts.

For practitioners using LLMs in academic translation, our findings suggest that careful selection of models based on text characteristics is crucial. DeepSeek-V3 may be preferable for texts requiring consistent overall quality, while GPT-4o might offer advantages for texts where syntactic complexity and lexical richness are valued. Our results also suggest potential benefits in combining the strengths of different models. Practical workflows could leverage DeepSeek-V3's overall quality while selectively incorporating GPT-4o's syntactic capabilities for specific text types or sections. Research into effective human-AI collaboration protocols for academic translation could maximize the strengths of both human translators and various LLMs.

However, this study has several limitations that should be acknowledged. The sample size for discourse-level assessment is limited to 11 texts, which might explain why some of the discourse-level assessments did not reach statistical significance. Additionally, our analysis focused on non-reasoning models, which may not represent the full capabilities of the latest LLM-powered systems.

In future studies, we plan to increase the number of texts analyzed to strengthen the statistical power of our discourse-level assessments. We also intend to further investigate reasoning-capable models such as DeepSeek-R1 and ChatGPT-4.5, which may demonstrate different translation strategies and capabilities. Further investigation into how reasoning capabilities affect translation fidelity and creativity could inform model selection and development for different translation needs. Moreover, incorporating human evaluation by native speakers of simplified Chinese would provide valuable insights into the perceived naturalness and acceptability of translations with different lexical diversity and syntactic complexity profiles.

In conclusion, this study reveals an interesting integration of automatic quality estimation scores and linguistic complexity metrics in LLM-powered translation. While DeepSeek-V3 achieves higher COMET scores, GPT-4o produces translations with greater lexical diversity and syntactic complexity. These findings suggest that different evaluation methods may capture different aspects of translation quality, highlighting the need for comprehensive assessment approaches that combine automatic metrics, linguistic analysis, and human evaluation to effectively leverage LLMs for specialized translation tasks. This extends beyond the specific models evaluated, which also applies to quality assessment of translations generated by other LLMs and commercial neural machine translation systems.

References

Abhaya Agarwal and Alon Lavie. 2008. Meteor, m-bleu and m-ter: Evaluation metrics for high-correlation with human rankings of machine translation output. In *Proceedings of the Third Workshop on Statistical Machine Translation*, pages 115–118.

Hadeel M Al-Smadi. 2022. Challenges in translating scientific texts: Problems and reasons. *Journal of language teaching and research*, 13(3):550–560.

Yuri Bizzoni, Tom S Juzek, Cristina España-Bonet, Koel Dutta Chowdhury, Josef van Genabith, and Elke Teich. 2020. How human is machine translationese? comparing human and machine translations of text and speech. In *Proceedings of the 17th International conference on spoken language translation*, pages 280–290.

Philippe Blache. 2011a. A computational model for linguistic complexity. In *Biology, Computation and Linguistics*, pages 155–167. IOS Press.

Philippe Blache. 2011b. Evaluating language complexity in context: New parameters for a constraint-based model. In *CSLP-11, workshop on constraint solving and language processing*. Citeseer.

Mojca Brglez and Špela Vintar. 2022. Lexical diversity in statistical and neural machine translation. *Information*, 13(2):93.

Sheila Castilho, Clodagh Quinn Mallon, Rahel Meister, and Shengya Yue. 2023. Do online machine translation systems care for context? what about a GPT model? In *Proceedings of the 24th Annual Conference of the European Association for Machine Translation (EAMT)*, pages 393–417.

Marie-Catherine De Marneffe, Christopher D Manning, Joakim Nivre, and Daniel Zeman. 2021. Universal dependencies. *Computational linguistics*, 47(2):255–308.

Jing Fang. 2020. Pause in sight translation: a pilot study. *Translation Education: A Tribute to the Establishment of World Interpreter and Translator Training Association (WITTA)*, pages 173–192.

Rudolf Flesch. 1979. How to write plain english. *University of Canterbury. Available at http://www. mang. canterbury. ac. nz/writing_guide/writing/flesch. shtml.[Retrieved 5 February 2016]*.

Yingxue Fu and Mark-Jan Nederhof. 2021. Automatic classification of human translation and machine translation: A study from the perspective of lexical diversity. *arXiv preprint arXiv:2105.04616*.

Edward Gibson. 1998. Linguistic complexity: Locality of syntactic dependencies. *Cognition*, 68(1):1–76.

Edward Gibson et al. 2000. The dependency locality theory: A distance-based theory of linguistic complexity. *Image, language, brain*, 2000:95–126.

Arthur C Graesser, Danielle S McNamara, and Jonna M Kulikowich. 2011. Coh-metrix: Providing multilevel analyses of text characteristics. *Educational researcher*, 40(5):223–234.

Zhiwei He, Tian Liang, Wenxiang Jiao, Zhuosheng Zhang, Yujiu Yang, Rui Wang, Zhaopeng Tu, Shuming Shi, and Xing Wang. 2024. Exploring human-like translation strategy with large language models. *Transactions of the Association for Computational Linguistics*, 12:229–246.

Wenxiang Jiao, Wenxuan Wang, Jen-tse Huang, Xing Wang, Shuming Shi, and Zhaopeng Tu. 2023. Is chatgpt a good translator? yes with gpt-4 as the engine. *arXiv preprint arXiv:2301.08745*.

Hoonmil Kim. 2020. The effects of lexical diversity and lexical sophistication of english on korean-english translation. *The Journal of Translation Studies ()*, 21(2):43–65.

Tom Kocmi, Eleftherios Avramidis, Rachel Bawden, Ondřej Bojar, Anton Dvorkovich, Christian Federmann, Mark Fishel, Markus Freitag, Thamme Gowda, Roman Grundkiewicz, et al. 2024. Findings of the wmt24 general machine translation shared task: the llm era is here but mt is not solved yet. In *Proceedings of the Ninth Conference on Machine Translation*, pages 1–46.

Rie Koizumi. 2012. Relationships between text length and lexical diversity measures: Can we use short texts of less than 100 tokens? *Vocabulary Learning and Instruction*, 1(1):60–69.

Alexandre Lacoste, Alexandra Luccioni, Victor Schmidt, and Thomas Dandres. 2019. Quantifying the carbon emissions of machine learning. *arXiv preprint arXiv:1910.09700*.

Aixin Liu, Bei Feng, Bing Xue, Bingxuan Wang, Bochao Wu, Chengda Lu, Chenggang Zhao, Chengqi Deng, Chenyu Zhang, Chong Ruan, et al. 2024. Deepseek-v3 technical report. *arXiv preprint arXiv:2412.19437*.

Jiacheng Liu, Ramakanth Pasunuru, Hannaneh Hajishirzi, Yejin Choi, and Asli Celikyilmaz. 2023. Crystal: Introspective reasoners reinforced with self-feedback. *arXiv preprint arXiv:2310.04921*.

Kanglong Liu, Zhongzhu Liu, and Lei Lei. 2022. Simplification in translated chinese: An entropy-based approach. *Lingua*, 275:103364.

Philip M McCarthy. 2005. *An assessment of the range and usefulness of lexical diversity measures and the potential of the measure of textual, lexical diversity (MTLD)*. Ph.D. thesis, The University of Memphis.

Danielle S McNamara, Arthur C Graesser, Philip M McCarthy, and Zhiqiang Cai. 2014. *Automated evaluation of text and discourse with Coh-Metrix*. Cambridge University Press.

Richard Moot and Christian Retoré. 2012. *The logic of categorial grammars: a deductive account of natural language syntax and semantics*, volume 6850. Springer.

OpenAI. 2025. Introducing GPT-4.5. OpenAI Website. Accessed: April 26, 2025.

Paperpal. 2023. How to make translating academic papers less challenging. Paperpal Blog. Accessed: April 26, 2025.

Kishore Papineni, Salim Roukos, Todd Ward, and Wei-Jing Zhu. 2002. Bleu: a method for automatic evaluation of machine translation. In *Proceedings of the 40th annual meeting of the Association for Computational Linguistics*, pages 311–318.

Peng Qi, Yuhao Zhang, Yuhui Zhang, Jason Bolton, and Christopher D Manning. 2020. Stanza: A python natural language processing toolkit for many human languages. *arXiv preprint arXiv:2003.07082*.

Vikas Raunak, Arul Menezes, Matt Post, and Hany Hassan Awadalla. 2023. Do gpts produce less literal translations? *arXiv preprint arXiv:2305.16806*.

Ricardo Rei, José GC De Souza, Duarte Alves, Chrysoula Zerva, Ana C Farinha, Taisiya Glushkova, Alon Lavie, Luisa Coheur, and André FT Martins. 2022. Comet-22: Unbabel-ist 2022 submission for the metrics shared task. In *Proceedings of the Seventh Conference on Machine Translation (WMT)*, pages 578–585.

Claude E Shannon. 1948. A mathematical theory of communication. *The Bell system technical journal*, 27(3):379–423.

Y Shi, H Xu, HL Kwok, and K Liu. 2024. Chatgpt in professional translation: A double-edged sword—insights from chinese translators on capabilities, concerns, and future prospects. *Translation and Interpreting in the Age of Artificial Intelligence. London/New York: Routledge*, page 2.

Slator. 2024. Experts weigh in on deepseek ai translation quality. Slator. Accessed: April 26, 2025.

Antonio Toral. 2019. Post-editese: an exacerbated translationese. *arXiv preprint arXiv:1907.00900*.

Eva Vanmassenhove, Dimitar Shterionov, and Matthew Gwilliam. 2021. Machine translationese: Effects of algorithmic bias on linguistic complexity in machine translation. *arXiv preprint arXiv:2102.00287*.

Longyue Wang, Chenyang Lyu, Tianbo Ji, Zhirui Zhang, Dian Yu, Shuming Shi, and Zhaopeng Tu. 2023. Document-level machine translation with large language models. *arXiv preprint arXiv:2304.02210*.

Lei Yu. 2024. ChatGPT [lexical diversity and syntactic complexity in ChatGPT translation]. *Foreign Language Teaching and Research ()*, 56(2):297–307.

Longhui Zou. 2024. *Cognitive Processes in Human-ChatGPT Interaction during Machine Translation Post-editing*. Ph.D. thesis, Kent State University.

Longhui Zou, Michael Carl, Mehdi Mirzapour, Hélène Jacquenet, and Lucas Nunes Vieira. 2021. Ai-based syntactic complexity metrics and sight interpreting performance. In *International Conference on Intelligent Human Computer Interaction*, pages 534–547. Springer.

Longhui Zou, Michael Carl, Shaghayegh Momtaz, and Mehdi Mirzapour. 2024. Impact of syntactic complexity on the processes and performance of large language models-leveraged post-editing. In *Proceedings of the 16th Conference of the Association for Machine Translation in the Americas (Volume 2: User Track)*, pages 259–260.

Sustainability Statement

CO2 Emission Related to Experiments

Experiments were conducted using Google Cloud Platform in region us-east1, which has a carbon efficiency of 0.37 kgCO_2eq/kWh. A cumulative of 120 hours of computation was performed on hardware of type A100 PCIe 40/80GB (TDP of 250W).

Total emissions are estimated to be 11.1 kgCO_2eq of which 100 percents were directly offset by the cloud provider.

Estimations were conducted using the Machine-Learning Impact calculator presented in (Lacoste et al., 2019).

Tailoring Machine Translation for Scientific Literature through Topic Filtering and Fuzzy Match Augmentation

Thomas Moerman[1], **Tom Vanallemeersch**[2], **Sara Szoc**[2] and **Arda Tezcan**[1]

[1]Language and Translation Technology Team (LT[3]), Ghent University
[2]CrossLang

Correspondence: {thomas.moerman,arda.tezcan}@ugent.be, {tom.vanallemeersch,sara.szoc}@crosslang.com

Abstract

To enhance the accessibility of scientific literature in multiple languages and facilitate the exchange of information among scholars and a wider audience, there is a need for high-performing specialized machine translation (MT) engines. However, this requires efficient filtering and the use of domain-specific data. This study examines whether translation quality improves when we increase training data through combining two methods: (1) data selection via topic filtering to identify relevant sentences from larger corpora, and (2) more efficient use of data by exploiting fuzzy matches (similar translations to a given input). We apply these techniques both to sequence-to-sequence MT models and off-the-shelf multilingual large language models (LLMs) in three scientific disciplines, namely neuroscience, climatology and mobility. Our results suggest that the combination of topic filtering and FM augmentation is an effective strategy for training neural machine translation (NMT) models from scratch, not only surpassing baseline NMT models but also delivering improved translation performance compared to smaller LLMs in terms of the number of parameters. Furthermore, we find that although FM augmentation through in-context learning generally improves LLM translation performance, limited domain-specific datasets can yield results comparable to those achieved with additional multi-domain datasets.

1 Introduction

The use of a lingua franca like English for scholarly communication is, on the one hand, beneficial as it facilitates knowledge dissemination to a certain extent in the international research landscape. On the other hand, it leads to inequalities among researchers (in terms of understanding and writing) and scientific information written in different languages reaches a limited audience (Ramírez-Castañeda, 2020; Bitetti and Ferreras, 2017). Machine translation (MT) is an important support for mitigating this problem and improving knowledge dissemination. For instance, with the support of MT systems, providing translations of abstracts, keywords, and full articles could become standard practice for research programs spanning multiple languages (Amano et al., 2021). More broadly, adopting translation as a standard practice could improve access to scientific research for scientists, students, educators, policymakers, journalists, and society as a whole (Steigerwald et al., 2022).

Translating scientific texts is challenging due to specialized terminology, complex syntax, domain-specific discourse, and the fluid boundaries of scientific disciplines (Byrne, 2014). Moreover, these unique characteristics of scientific literature and the limited language resources for training MT systems further complicate the task for such systems. In the Translations and Open Science project (Fiorini et al., 2023), which we refer to henceforth as *TaOS*, custom MT engines were trained for various scientific disciplines. This effort showed that it is challenging to collect parallel training data for scientific disciplines, as many texts are only available in one language (translation is not an activity that is habitually applied in scholarly communication because of disciplinary standards and because there is a shortage of human resources).

In this paper, we approach the scarcity of scientifically oriented parallel training data for the English→French language direction by (1) applying data selection (using topic-based classifiers) to efficiently filter larger corpora in order to identify potentially relevant training material for building sequence-to-sequence neural MT (NMT) models from scratch, and (2) exploiting fuzzy match (FM) augmentation techniques (i.e. leveraging the translation of sentences similar to a given input) to make more efficient use of the available data for

Proceedings of the Eleventh Workshop on Patent and Scientific Literature Translation (PSLT 2025), pages 13–26, June 24, 2025

NMT models as well as off-the-shelf LLMs. In this study, we mainly focus on training NMT models from scratch and less to LLMs for various reasons: LLMs (the training data of which are typically unknown) may present data leakage and thus suffer from unrepresentative evaluations; they require more substantial computational infrastructure for inference (NMT models can run on CPU, whereas this is far less obvious for LLM models); and finally, the answers of instruct variants of LLMs need some post-processing. Therefore, we do not provide a comprehensive comparison between (pre-trained) NMT models and LLMs: while fine-tuning pre-trained NMT models and LLMs are common and effective, we merely focus on out-of-the-box translation capabilities of LLMs (i.e. zero-shot) and through in-context learning.

2 Related Research

2.1 NMT and LLMs in Specialized Domains

Advancements in NMT, driven mainly by adopting the transformer architecture (Vaswani et al., 2017a), have greatly enhanced translation quality across various domains. In recent years, further improvements have been achieved in MT performance with LLMs, which leverage extensive training data and advanced architectures and enhance translation accuracy, fluency, and adaptability across diverse contexts. While LLMs have consistently outperformed traditional models in general-domain MT tasks in recent years, such as for news, literary texts, and social media (Kocmi et al., 2023, 2024), their effectiveness in specialized domains remains less conclusive. In the WMT 2024 patent translation task, transformer-based NMT systems from previous years (2019 and 2020) achieved the best translation performance as measured by automatic evaluation metrics for multiple language pairs (Higashiyama, 2024). Furthermore, a recent study by Wassie et al. (2025) shows that even large fine-tuned LLMs underperform compared to transformer-based multilingual encoder-decoder models when trained on domain-specific medical translation data. These findings highlight the importance of assessing the performance of NMT systems alongside LLMs for domain-specific MT, as traditional NMT models may still offer competitive or even superior performance in such scenarios.

2.2 Science-oriented Data and NMT Models

To address the lack of parallel data for scientific texts in underrepresented European languages, the SciPar corpus was created and made publicly available through the ELRC-SHARE repository (Roussis et al., 2022). Additionally, as part of the TaOS project we mentioned earlier, Fiorini et al. (2023) compiled 316,701 parallel sentences across three scientific disciplines: (i) Climatology and Climate Change (code PE10 in the European Research Council nomenclature), (ii) Neuroscience and Disorders of the Nervous System (LS5), and (iii) Human Mobility, Environment, and Space (SH7). The sentences originated from several publication types, such as journal articles, journal article abstracts and thesis abstracts). In a more recent effort, Roussis et al. (2024) collected approximately 11 million sentence pairs for English-Spanish, English-Portuguese, and English-French from 62 academic repositories, covering Cancer Research, Energy Research, Neuroscience, Transportation Research, and general academic texts (this dataset is not publicly available).

Efforts have also been made to develop MT systems for scientific literature. In the TaOS project, NMT engines were trained for the three abovementioned scientific disciplines for the language directions English→French and French→English. The engines were trained using a combination of publicly available corpora covering a variety of domains and the abovementioned compiled sentences. The results were evaluated by various *personas*, i.e. professional translators, researchers, and students without specific knowledge of the disciplines in question. Both automatic and human evaluation showed that the specialized engines have a substantially better translation quality than the baseline, i.e. engines merely trained on the public corpora. Similarly, Roussis et al. applied domain adaptation by fine-tuning a pre-trained NMT model (OPUS-MT) for the language directions Spanish→English, Portuguese→English, and French→English, demonstrating that scientific texts enhance MT performance according to automatic evaluation metrics.

2.3 Data Selection for NMT

In order to increase the amount of domain-specific training data, various data selection approaches can be applied to corpora that cover a variety of topics. An overview of data selection techniques for domain adaptation in NMT can be found in Chu and Wang (2018). One possible approach is to create classifiers that are trained on data belonging to a domain (positive examples) and data not belonging to it (negative examples) and to extract potentially relevant training sentences from other corpora, as illustrated by Defauw et al. (2019). Other potential approaches consist of comparing sentences between the multi-domain corpora and domain-specific resources using metrics like embedding similarity, see e.g. Pourmostafa et al. (2021), or the application of topic clustering to sentences, for instance using Latent Dirichlet Allocation (Blei et al., 2001).

2.4 FM Augmentation for NMT and LLMs

Numerous approaches have been implemented to enhance domain-specific NMT performance by leveraging FMs from bilingual resources in the given domain. Some methods modify transformer-based architectures by adjusting the decoding process (Cao and Xiong, 2018; Reheman et al., 2023), integrating lexical memory into the NMT architecture (Feng et al., 2017), introducing additional attention layers to capture information from translation memories (TMs) (He et al., 2021), or proposing a new architecture that can effectively edit FMs to produce MT output (Bouthors et al., 2023). FMs have also been effectively integrated into NMT through data augmentation; they leverage source text similarity to retrieve FMs and incorporate them by augmenting the source sentences in training, validation and test datasets (Xu et al., 2020; Tezcan et al., 2021). This approach has proven particularly effective in specialized domains starting from training sets of approximately 300K sentence pairs, with further improvements observed for larger datasets (Tezcan et al., 2024).

FM augmentation approaches do not only enhance NMT performance. LLMs have also shown the ability to leverage FMs in domain-specific scenarios through in-context learning: highly similar FMs are added to a given input sentence in LLM prompts, enabling the LLM to replicate previously observed translation patterns (Moslem et al., 2023a; Mu et al., 2023). Furthermore, incorporating FMs (Moslem et al., 2023b) or randomly selected examples from domain-specific datasets (Alves et al., 2023) into the fine-tuning process, alongside input prompts has been shown to enhance the MT performance of LLMs.

3 Methodology

3.1 Data Selection

We performed topic filtering by applying science-oriented classifiers that extract potentially relevant training sentences from other corpora. A classifier determines how likely a target-language sentence originates from a scientific discipline. We used the FastText tool[1] to create classifiers based on the target-language part of discipline-specific TaOS training data (the positive examples consist of a random sample of sentences from one discipline, and the negative examples originate from the two other disciplines). When applying the classifier to an unseen sentence, we required a minimal score to accept it as an example of the class. This score is the lowest score observed at the best trade-off point of the ROC curve for the training examples, i.e. the point where the formula $TPR - FPR$ (true positive ratio minus false positive ratio) reaches its maximum.

We applied the classifiers to corpora covering various scientifically oriented and other topics. Given that the target-language sentences satisfy the minimal score, we retrieved the corresponding source-language sentences from the corpora and obtained additional sentence pairs to be used as NMT training data.

3.2 FM Augmentation

For FM retrieval, we followed the neural fuzzy repair (NFR) approach of Tezcan et al. (2021).[2] Given a bilingual dataset consisting of source/target sentence pairs S, T, for each source sentence $s_i \in S$ with the translations $\{t_1, \dots, t_n\} \in T$, we retrieved the n the most similar source sentences in the same dataset $\{s_1, \dots, s_n\} \in S$ (i.e., these are FMs), where $s_i \notin \{s_1, \dots, s_n\}$ (i.e. we excluded exact matches), given that the FM similarity score is above a fixed threshold: $\lambda \geq 0.5$. To this end, we measured the FM score $FM(s_i, s_j)$ between two source sentences s_i and s_j as the cosine similarity between their sentence embeddings e_i and e_j:

$$FM(s_i, s_j) = \frac{e_i \cdot e_j}{\|e_i\| \times \|e_j\|} \quad (1)$$

where $\|e\|$ is the magnitude of vector e.

We generated the sentence embeddings using sent2vec (Pagliardini et al., 2018), while we effi-

[1] https://fasttext.cc/

[2] https://github.com/lt3/nfr

ciently retrieved FMs using a FAISS index (Johnson et al., 2021). The hyperparameters for sentence embedding generation and FAISS index construction are detailed in Appendices A.2 and A.3, respectively. Before FM retrieval, all sentences were segmented into subwords using SentencePiece (Kudo and Richardson, 2018), more specifically using the XLM-RoBERTa (base) tokenizer.[3] Table 1 illustrates the FM retrieval process.

S	We **found three** studies for inclusion in the review.
$score$	0.9309
FM_S	We **identified nine eligible** studies for inclusion in the review.
FM_T	Nous avons **identifié neuf** études **éligibles** pour l'inclusion dans la revue.
T	Nous avons **trouvé trois** études pour l'inclusion dans la revue.

Table 1: An example of FM retrieval for the English→French language direction in the neuroscience discipline for a given source sentence S and the reference translation T. FM_S and FM_T refer to the source and target sides of the retrieved FM with the FM similarity score, which is indicated as $score$. The non-matching parts are marked in bold.

The work of Tezcan et al. (2021) demonstrated that, in the context of transformer-based NMT systems, the augmentation of a given source sentence with the best FM yields notable improvements in MT performance but the effectiveness of incorporating additional FMs is less clear. Following this work, for the NMT systems, FM augmentation was implemented using (only) the best FM (i.e. FM with the highest similarity score), where FM-augmented source sentences S^* consist of the original source sentence, concatenated by the translation of the retrieved FM, using a separator token (S *<sep>* FM_T). The training data consists of both the original and the FM-augmented source/target sentence pairs S, T and S^*, T, respectively. During inference (i.e. on the test and validation sets), each source sentence is augmented using the same FM retrieval method described earlier. If no FMs are retrieved above the threshold $\lambda \geq 0.5$, the original (non-augmented) source sentence is used as input to the FM-augmented NMT model.

FM augmentation for LLM experiments is implemented by adding n-best FM_S/FM_T pairs to the instruction prompts to leverage the in-context learning abilities of the given LLM alongside the input sentence S for which the MT output is produced. The prompt templates are provided in Appendix A.6.

4 Experimental Setup

4.1 Data

We randomly split the TaOS data[4] for the three disciplines into training, validation, and test sets, ensuring that there is no overlap between them in terms of sentence pairs. The maximum number of tokens per sentence (prior to sub-word tokenization) in all partitions was limited to a maximum of 100. Additionally, sentences consisting of a single token were removed in the validation and test sets. Finally, we ensured that there were no unaligned sentence pairs (i.e. sentence pairs with very low translation equivalence) by analyzing the source-target pairs in the validation and test sets using the SentenceTransformer model LaBSE[5] (Feng et al., 2022) setting a minimum equivalence score of 0.6. The number of sentence pairs in the final partitions are provided in Table 2 while the average token count for each dataset can be found in Appendix A.1.

	Train	Validation	Test
Neuroscience	98,857	1,552	1,543
Climatology	95,694	1,630	1,609
Mobility	106,282	1,784	1,752

Table 2: The number of sentences partitioned from the TaOS data as training, validation and test sets per discipline.

In order to generate additional MT training data, we first created a classifier for each of the three disciplines in the TaOS data, using the method described in 3.1. We then applied these classifiers to the French sentences in the three below multi-domain corpora, filtered out low-scoring sentences, and retrieved their English pendant to obtain a set of sentence pairs:

- SciPar:[6] a collection of parallel corpora from scientific abstracts;
- EuroPat:[7] a parallel corpus of European patent data;

[3] https://huggingface.co/docs/transformers/v4.22.2/en/model_doc/xlm-roberta#overview

[4] The data supporting the findings of this study are available upon request by contacting the corresponding author(s). The data are provided for research purposes only.

[5] https://huggingface.co/sentence-transformers/LaBSE

[6] https://opus.nlpl.eu/ELRC-5067-SciPar/en&es/v1/ELRC-5067-SciPar

[7] https://europat.net/ and https://opus.nlpl.eu/EuroPat/en&fr/v3/EuroPat

- ParaCrawl:[8] a parallel data set extracted from a large set of downloaded web pages.

Before applying the classifiers, we filtered out additional sentences from the three datasets using the following approaches:

- We filtered out sentences with a low translation equivalence using the LaBSE model setting a minumum equivalence score of 0.6, as the construction of these corpora involved automated alignment, which sometimes leads to sentence pairs that are not or are only partially equivalent[9]. We only applied the equivalence detection to a 10M sample of ParaCrawl because of the high computation cost; therefore, the topic filtering is only applied to this sample.
- We filtered out short sentences (less than 10 words).

The number of sentence pairs used from the additional datasets are provided in Table 3.

	Europat	ParaCrawl	SciPar
Original	11,032,300	9,765,499	1,063,329
TF Neurosci.	2,156,482	2,508,710	392,037
TF Climat.	6,998,414	2,713,013	474,472
TF Mobility	2,610,923	5,879,689	334,144

Table 3: The number of sentence pairs used as additional training data for the NMT systems and for FM augmentation (for both NMT and LLM experiments), obtained from three datasets, before and after topic filtering (indicated as *Original* and *TF*, respectively), per discipline.

4.2 NMT Models

We trained NMT models from scratch, using configurations varying on two aspects: (i) training data and (ii) FM augmentation. All systems utilized validation sets for the given scientific discipline (i.e. neuroscience, climatology, or mobility).

Regarding the first aspect, we tested the following training data configurations:

- *1d*: TaOS data for a given discipline;
- *3d*: all TaOS data (i.e. combination of all three disciplines);
- *3d+Ext*: all TaOS data combined with all extra (i.e. *original*) multi-domain datasets (i.e. ParaCrawl, EuroPat and SciPar);
- *3d+ExtTF*: all TaOS data combined with the results of topic filtering (*TF*), as described in Section 3.1, on the extra datasets for the given discipline.

Regarding the second aspect, the above configurations were combined with FM augmentation[10], as described in Section 3.2. This increases the size of the training data for all configurations.

An overview of the training set sizes of the configurations is provided in Appendix A.4. All the NMT systems trained from these datasets utilized the transformer architecture (Vaswani et al., 2017b) and the OpenNMT-py toolkit[11] (Klein et al., 2017). Prior to training, all sentences were segmented into sub-words using SentencePiece, as described in Section 3.2. The resulting vocabulary sizes per system are provided in Appendix A.4. All systems were trained with shuffled training datasets and early stopping with 10 validation rounds in terms of accuracy and perplexity. All training runs were initialized with the same seed. For the systems that do not utilize FM augmentation, the maximum source and target lengths were set to 200 tokens. The maximum source length was doubled to 400 tokens for the systems that utilize FM augmentation. Other details regarding the hyper-parameters used for training the NMT systems are provided in Appendix A.5.

4.3 LLMs

We utilized LLMs in zero-shot and FM-augmented settings through in-context learning. We tested four models: Mistral 7B (base)[12] and 24B (instruct)[13] (Jiang et al., 2023), Tower 7B (instruct)[14] (Alves et al., 2024), which was fine-tuned on Mistral for translation-related tasks, and Mistral Nemo 12B (instruct).[15] The *instruct* variants were necessary in case of the larger models, as they proved more suitable for translation tasks without additional fine-tuning steps.

We tested two types of prompting strategies: (i) a zero-shot setting with a simple translation instruction, and (ii) a 12-shot setting, following the work of (2023a), in which prompts were augmented with

[8] `https://paracrawl.eu/` and `https://opus.nlpl.eu/ParaCrawl/corpus/version/ParaCrawl`

[9] Based on the test sets held out from the TaOS data, it appeared that virtually all sentences minimally had this score.

[10] As an exception, due to the limited size of the *1d* training sets, we did not apply further FM augmentation for this configuration.

[11] `https://github.com/OpenNMT/OpenNMT-py`, v. 3.5.1.

[12] `https://huggingface.co/mistralai/Mistral-7B-v0.3`

[13] `https://huggingface.co/mistralai/Mistral-Small-24B-Instruct-2501`

[14] `https://huggingface.co/Unbabel/TowerInstruct-Mistral-7B-v0.2`

[15] `https://huggingface.co/mistralai/Mistral-Nemo-Instruct-2407`

12-best FMs (source/target pairs), as described in Section 3.2. To test the usefulness of FM augmentation in different data configurations, FMs were retrieved from the four different training datasets used for NMT training, i.e. *1d*, *3d*, *Ext* and *ExtTF*.

4.4 Evaluation

We made use of the automated evaluation metrics SacreBLEU,[16] (Post, 2018), chrF (Popović, 2015), and COMET[17] (Rei et al., 2020) to assess the quality of the (detokenized) MT output. To verify whether differences between the automated quality metric scores of the different MT systems are statistically significant, we used bootstrap resampling tests (Koehn, 2004). We performed both the automated evaluations and bootstrap resampling tests using the MATEO toolkit[18] (Vanroy et al., 2023), with the default settings for each metric.

5 Results

5.1 NMT Models

Table 4 provides the automated evaluation results for the translations generated by the different MT models on the discipline-specific test sets.

Examining the NMT models, we observe that increasing the training set size from single-discipline datasets (*1d*) to utilizing all available data from the three scientific disciplines, along with additional out-of-domain data (*3d_Ext*), positively impacted translation performance. Furthermore, applying topic filtering to the out-of-domain datasets (*ExtTF*) and incorporating FM augmentation (*FM*) further enhanced the automatic metric scores across all datasets and disciplines, highlighting the effectiveness of both techniques. The best-performing system leveraged the combined datasets from all three scientific disciplines with topic-filtered extra data (*3d+ExtTF_FM*) and FM augmentation, achieving statistically significant improvements over all other configurations. Notably, regarding the NMT experiments, FM augmentation proved most effective when paired with the dataset configuration that leveraged topic-filtered multi-domain datasets, delivering greater improvements than when applied to the full, unfiltered datasets.

[16]`https://github.com/mjpost/sacrebleu` v. 2.4.1. (SacreBLEU and chrF)

[17]`https://huggingface.co/Unbabel/wmt22-comet-da`

[18]`https://mateo.ivdnt.org/`

5.2 LLMs

When analyzing the results across different LLMs, we can make multiple observations. Firstly, FM augmentation through in-context learning enhanced the performance of all tested LLMs, across all metrics and disciplines, with one exception: Mistral Nemo 13B model generally achieved the highest automatic metric scores in zero-shot setting without FM augmentation. Secondly, the impact of the additional datasets is inconclusive for the Tower, Nemo, and Mistral 24B models, while FM augmentation improved performance. Expanding the pool of sentences in the limited discipline-specific datasets (i.e. *1d*) for FM retrieval, whether by merging training data from all three disciplines or incorporating additional multi-domain datasets with or without topic filtering, did not consistently lead to improvements or, at best, resulted in only marginal gains. For instance, the Mistral 24B model achieved the highest COMET scores in the climatology and mobility disciplines utilizing only the discipline-specific datasets for FM augmentation. It could be argued that given the additional computational resources required for extracting FMs from more extensive data sets, restricting the pool of sentences for FM retrieval to the given scientific discipline (using approximately 100K sentences) offers a more favourable balance between efficiency and quality. Please also see Figure 1 for an overview of the best-performing configuration per model and discipline.

When comparing different LLMs, we observe that the translation performances of the general-purpose models (e.g., Mistral, Mistral Nemo) improved with the increasing number of parameters. The Tower 7B models deviated from this general pattern, outperforming the smaller Mistral 7B models using the same data configurations, as well as the larger Nemo 13B models across all metrics and disciplines. These results confirm the effectiveness of the Tower model compared to other LLMs of similar size in the MT task (Kocmi et al., 2024). In the context of LLM parameter size, it should also be highlighted that although the larger models generally resulted in higher scores, the smallest Mistral model (7B) achieved the highest relative gains from FM augmentation compared to the zero-shot setting. For instance, in the neuroscience discipline, *Mistral 7B_FM_3d+ExtTF* outperforms *Mistral 7B* by +2.78 COMET, whereas *Mistral*

	Neuroscience			Climatology			Mobility		
NMT model	BLEU	chrF	COMET	BLEU	chrF	COMET	BLEU	chrF	COMET
1d	39.11	65.15	79.28	29.57	57.99	76.05	30.14	59.45	76.98
3d	43.11	68.40	83.06	35.24	62.62	81.01	33.96	62.32	81.73
3d_FM	43.67	68.74	83.47	35.38	62.55	81.14	33.96	62.40	81.73
3d+Ext	44.40	69.42	84.70	35.70	63.35	82.48	36.11	64.01	84.88
3d+Ext_FM	44.78	69.58	85.12	36.32	63.54	82.79	36.09	63.96	84.80
3d+ExtTF	44.99	69.75	84.73	36.28	63.76	82.54	36.89	64.49	84.96
3d+ExtTF_FM	**46.33**‡	**70.58**‡	**85.30**†	**36.97**†	**64.00**†	**82.82**	**37.68**‡	**64.81***	**85.27**‡
LLM									
Mistral 7B	32.85	61.58	81.64	28.66	57.98	79.97	29.98	59.19	82.48
Mistral 7B_FM_1d	39.74	65.94	84.37	32.76	60.71	82.45	33.55	61.87	85.01
Mistral 7B_FM_3d	39.35	65.71	84.29	32.69	60.56	82.35	33.70	61.88	85.04
Mistral 7B_FM_3d+Ext	**40.72**	66.23	84.37	**34.79***	**61.90***	**82.76**	**35.35**	**62.73**	**85.11**
Mistral 7B_FM_3d+ExtTF	40.50	**66.28**	**84.42**	34.42	61.52	82.70	35.27	62.69	85.08
Tower 7B	40.81	66.55	84.74	34.28	61.92	82.77	36.18	63.19	85.02
Tower 7B_FM_1d	41.97	67.11	84.92	35.22	62.28	82.92	35.84	63.02	85.30
Tower 7B_FM_3d	41.98	67.11	84.90	35.03	62.16	82.84	35.92	63.08	85.36
Tower 7B_FM_3d+Ext	**43.17***	**67.74***	**84.95**	**36.68***	**62.91**	82.90	**37.08**	63.55	85.22
Tower 7B_FM_3d+ExtTF	42.82	67.53	84.93	36.43	62.84	**82.96**	36.99	**63.62**	**85.38**
Nemo 13B	40.04	**67.01***	**84.77**†	**33.58**	**62.31**†	**82.97**†	**34.55**	**63.16**†	**85.44**†
Nemo 13B_FM_1d	40.63	65.84	83.95	33.16	60.54	81.95	33.78	61.29	84.46
Nemo 13B_FM_3d	40.72	65.98	84.04	33.27	60.77	82.15	33.47	61.07	84.30
Nemo 13B_FM_3d+Ext	40.94	66.08	83.95	33.39	60.44	81.64	34.16	61.21	84.05
Nemo 13B_FM_3d+ExtTF	**41.05**	66.16	83.93	33.42	60.57	81.72	33.72	60.99	84.01
Mistral 24B	42.23	68.49	85.51	35.90	63.70	83.61	37.46	65.07	86.18
Mistral 24B_FM_1d	44.88	69.81	86.10	37.27	64.44	**84.13**	38.72	65.68	**86.72***
Mistral 24B_FM_3d	44.94	69.90	**86.18**	37.24	64.43	84.12	38.57	65.54	86.64
Mistral 24B_FM_3d+Ext	**45.08**	69.91	86.11	37.26	64.47	84.12	**38.85**	65.68	86.61
Mistral 24B_FM_3d+ExtTF	45.05	**69.92**	**86.18**	**37.31**	**64.51**	84.12	**38.85**	**65.69**	86.62

Table 4: Results of the automatic evaluations performed for the different MT systems, per discipline. For each model (i.e. per section), the highest metric scores are highlighted in bold and statistically significant improvements are denoted by $*$, $\dagger$, and $\ddagger$, representing $p < 0.05$, $p < 0.01$, and $p < 0.001$, respectively, based on the lowest p values obtained when compared to all other configurations of the same model type.

24B_FM_ExtTF shows an improvement of +0.67 COMET over *Mistral 24B*.

5.3 Cross-comparison

In a final analysis, we compare the performance of the best configuration per model type using COMET as the primary evaluation metric, with Figure 1 presenting the automated evaluation results per discipline of the single best-performing setup for each model type. This figure further includes the statistical significance of the performance differences observed between the various model types.

Upon reviewing the overall best-performing model, we observe that the largest LLM, Mistral 24B, surpassed all other models with respect to COMET scores, achieving an improvement of up to +1.26 within the mobility discipline compared to all other tested models. However, in the neuroscience discipline, the highest BLEU and chrF scores were attained by the top-performing NMT configuration (*3d+ExtTM_FM*), with improvements of +1.28 BLEU and +0.66 chrF compared to the best-performing LLM (Mistral 24B). Moreover, the best NMT configuration surpassed Mistral 7B, Tower 7B and Nemo 13B across all disciplines and metrics, with the exception of COMET scores in the climatology and mobility disciplines, where Tower 7B achieved higher scores. Since BLEU and chrF emphasize token and character overlap between the MT output and the reference translations, it can be hypothesized that while the NMT model is better at maintaining discipline-specific lexical choices for the neuroscience domain, the COMET scores, which measure semantic similarity, suggest that Tower 7B and Mistral 24B better capture the overall meaning. However, this hypothesis requires validation through manual evaluation and error analysis of MT performance in subsequent studies.

6 Conclusions and Future Work

Developing highly accurate MT systems for specialized scientific disciplines continues to be a significant challenge due to unique textual characteristics and the scarcity of language resources neces-

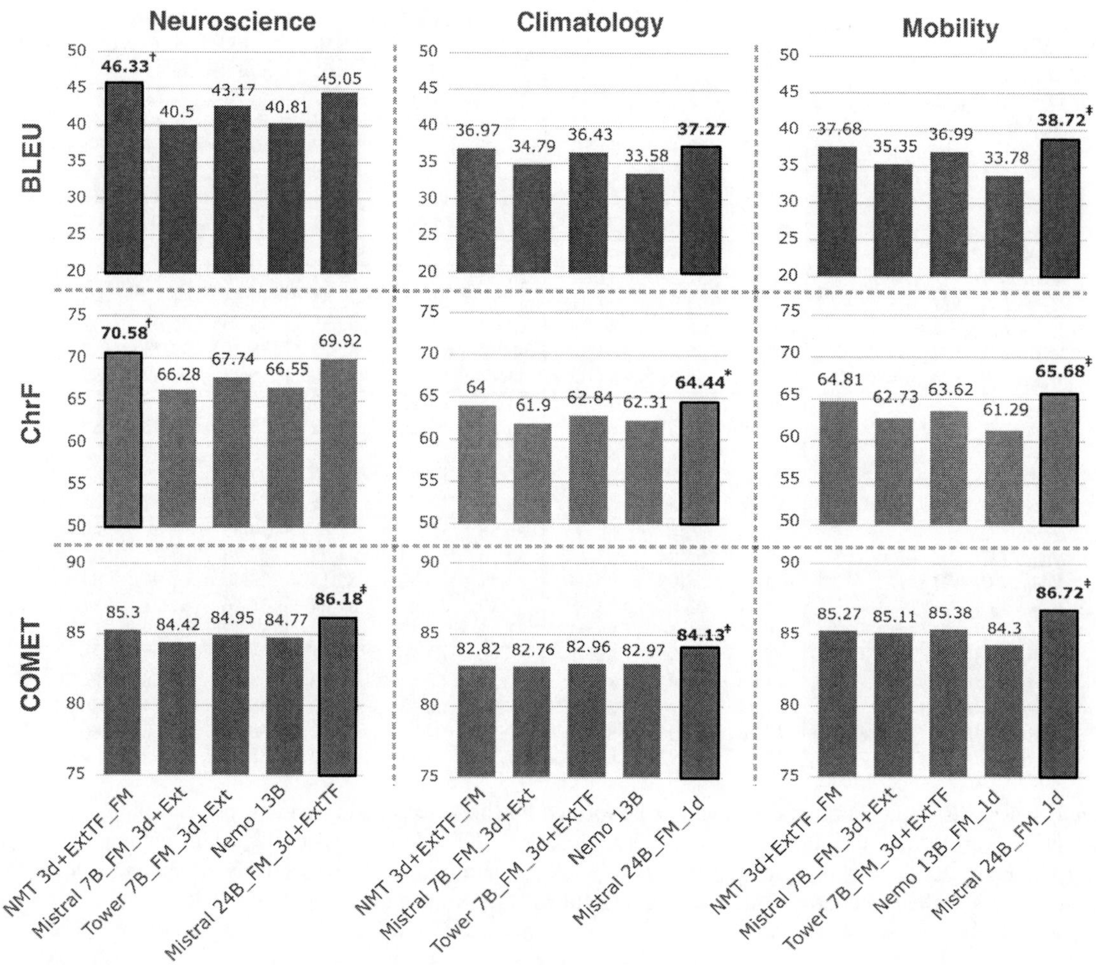

Figure 1: Results of the automatic evaluations for the best-performing configuration per model type selected in terms of COMET scores (NMT vs. LLMs), per discipline. The highest metric scores per metric and discipline are highlighted in bold and statistically significant improvements are denoted by *, †, and ‡, representing $p < 0.05$, $p < 0.01$, and $p < 0.001$, respectively, based on the lowest p values obtained when compared to all other models.

sary for building effective MT systems.

In this study, we combined two existing methodologies, aiming to tailor MT systems for the scientific domain, namely topic filtering of large, multi-domain datasets to extract relevant NMT training data and FM augmentation to utilize the available data more efficiently. To this end, we trained NMT models from scratch and employed four LLMs to evaluate their zero-shot and in-context learning capabilities. Our experiments, which covered three scientific disciplines, namely neuroscience, climatology, and mobility, in the English→French language direction, revealed that combining topic filtering with FM augmentation effectively enhances NMT models trained from scratch. However, although FM augmentation via in-context learning proved beneficial for most of the LLMs tested, the value of additional datasets in this context, regardless of whether they included topic filtering, remained inconclusive. Our findings suggest that smaller, discipline-specific datasets could yield comparable results to larger datasets when employed for FM augmentation in this specific setting, while incurring significantly lower computational costs.

Furthermore, our findings enable a comparison between NMT models trained from scratch and LLMs (without further fine-tuning) for this task. We demonstrated that specialized NMT models can achieve superior translation performance compared to out-of-the-box LLMs in this discipline-specific scenario, with these improvements being more pronounced when compared to smaller LLMs with fewer parameters. Therefore, it can be argued that these improvements in translation quality and other benefits, such as reduced inference costs, make NMT systems a viable option for translating scientific literature, particularly when computational resources are limited. However, given the positive correlation we observed between translation performance and the increasing number of LLM parameters, our findings suggest that larger LLMs, even in the absence of further fine-tuning, could deliver better translation performance than such specialized NMT models.

In future studies, we will test additional configurations with given datasets, for example, retrieving FMs for the test/validation sets only from the discipline-specific datasets while using extra, larger datasets as additional NMT training data and for FM augmentation on the training set. Moreover, we will investigate the effectiveness of additionally fine-tuning pre-trained NMT models and LLMs using the in-domain datasets, with or without FM augmentation (i.e. zero- vs. few-shot settings), as both approaches have been shown to further improve MT performance in previous studies.

7 Limitations

One of the main limitations of this study is its limited scope in terms of MT experiments, which do not explore fine-tuning strategies of pre-trained NMT models or LLMs. Moreover, our experiments were limited to automatic assessment of MT performance, which may not fully reflect translation quality, and to a single language pair, albeit across three scientific disciplines. Human evaluation of MT performance and additional experiments in different language directions would be necessary to validate our findings. Furthermore, our evaluation focused on the effectiveness of combining specific data selection and augmentation methods rather than comparing them against a wider range of alternative approaches. Finally, we did not explore the efficiency of different n values for integrating n-best FMs into the LLM prompts or additional prompting strategies.

Acknowledgments

The computational resources (Stevin Supercomputer Infrastructure) and services used in this work were provided by the VSC (Flemish Supercomputer Center), which is funded by Ghent University, FWO and the Flemish Government department EWI.

References

Duarte Alves, Nuno Guerreiro, João Alves, José Pombal, Ricardo Rei, José de Souza, Pierre Colombo, and Andre Martins. 2023. Steering large language models for machine translation with finetuning and in-context learning. In *Findings of the Association for Computational Linguistics: EMNLP 2023*, pages 11127–11148, Singapore. Association for Computational Linguistics.

Duarte M. Alves, José Pombal, Nuno M. Guerreiro, Pedro H. Martins, João Alves, Amin Farajian, Ben Peters, Ricardo Rei, Patrick Fernandes, Sweta Agrawal, Pierre Colombo, José G. C. de Souza, and André F. T. Martins. 2024. Tower: An open multilingual large language model for translation-related tasks. *Preprint*, arXiv:2402.17733.

Tatsuya Amano, Violeta Berdejo Espinola, Alec P. Christie, Kate Willott, Munemitsu Akasaka, András Báldi, Anna Berthinussen, Sandro Bertolino, Andrew J. Bladon, Min Chen, Chang-Yong Choi, Magda Bou Dagher Kharrat, Luis G. de Oliveira, Perla Farhat, Marina Golivets, Nataly Hidalgo Aranzamendi, Kerstin Jantke, Joanna Kajzer-Bonk, M. Çisel Kemahlı Aytekin, Igor Khorozyan, Kensuke Kito, Ko Konno, Da-Li Lin, Nick Littlewood, Yang Liu, Yifan Liu, Matthias-Claudio Loretto, Valentina Marconi, Philip Martin, William H. Morgan, Juan P. Narváez-Gómez, Pablo Jose Negret, Elham Nourani, Jose M. Ochoa Quintero, Nancy Ockendon, Rachel Rui Ying Oh, Silviu Petrovan, Ana C. Piovezan-Borges, Ingrid L. Pollet, Danielle L. Ramos, Ana L. Reboredo Segovia, A. Nayelli Rivera-Villanueva, Ricardo Rocha, Marie-Morgane Rouyer, Katherine A. Sainsbury, Richard Schuster, Dominik Schwab, Çağan H. Şekercioğlu, Hemin Seo, Gorm Shackelford, Yushin Shinoda, Rebecca K. Smith, Shan-dar Tao, Ming-shan Tsai, Elizabeth Tyler, Flóra Vajna, José Osvaldo Valdebenito, Svetlana Vozykova, Paweł Waryszak, Veronica Zamora-Gutierrez, Rafael D. Zenni, Wenjun Zhou, and William J. Sutherland. 2021. Tapping into non-english-language science for the conservation of global biodiversity. *bioRxiv*.

Mario Santiago Di Bitetti and Julián A. Ferreras. 2017. Publish (in english) or perish: The effect on citation rate of using languages other than english in scientific publications. *Ambio*, 46:121–127.

David Blei, Andrew Ng, and Michael Jordan. 2001. Latent dirichlet allocation. In *Advances in Neural Information Processing Systems*, volume 14. MIT Press.

Maxime Bouthors, Josep Crego, and François Yvon. 2023. Towards example-based NMT with multi-Levenshtein transformers. In *Proceedings of the 2023 Conference on Empirical Methods in Natural Language Processing*, pages 1830–1846, Singapore. Association for Computational Linguistics.

Jody Byrne. 2014. *Scientific and technical translation explained: A nuts and bolts guide for beginners*. Routledge.

Qian Cao and Deyi Xiong. 2018. Encoding gated translation memory into neural machine translation. In *Proceedings of the 2018 Conference on Empirical Methods in Natural Language Processing*, pages 3042–3047.

Chenhui Chu and Rui Wang. 2018. A survey of domain adaptation for neural machine translation. In *Proceedings of the 27th International Conference on Computational Linguistics*, pages 1304–1319, Santa Fe, New Mexico, USA. Association for Computational Linguistics.

Arne Defauw, Tom Vanallemeersch, Sara Szoc, Frederic Everaert, Koen Van Winckel, Kim Scholte, Joris Brabers, and Joachim Van den Bogaert. 2019. Collecting domain specific data for MT: an evaluation of the ParaCrawl pipeline. In *Proceedings of Machine Translation Summit XVII: Translator, Project and User Tracks*, pages 186–195, Dublin, Ireland. European Association for Machine Translation.

Fangxiaoyu Feng, Yinfei Yang, Daniel Cer, Naveen Arivazhagan, and Wei Wang. 2022. Language-agnostic BERT sentence embedding. In *Proceedings of the 60th Annual Meeting of the Association for Computational Linguistics (Volume 1: Long Papers)*, pages 878–891, Dublin, Ireland. Association for Computational Linguistics.

Yang Feng, Shiyue Zhang, Andi Zhang, Dong Wang, and Andrew Abel. 2017. Memory-augmented neural machine translation. In *Proceedings of the 2017 Conference on Empirical Methods in Natural Language Processing*, pages 1390–1399, Copenhagen, Denmark. Association for Computational Linguistics.

Susanna Fiorini, Arda Tezcan, Tom Vanallemeersch, Sara Szoc, Kristin Migdisi, Laurens Meeus, and Lieve Macken. 2023. Translations and open science: exploring how translation technologies can support multilingualism in scholarly communication. In *Proceedings of the International Conference HiT-IT 2023*, pages 41–51. INCOMA Ltd.

Qiuxiang He, Guoping Huang, Qu Cui, Li Li, and Lemao Liu. 2021. Fast and accurate neural machine translation with translation memory. In *Proceedings of the 59th Annual Meeting of the Association for Computational Linguistics and the 11th International Joint Conference on Natural Language Processing (Volume 1: Long Papers)*, pages 3170–3180, Online. Association for Computational Linguistics.

Shohei Higashiyama. 2024. Results of the WAT/WMT 2024 shared task on patent translation. In *Proceedings of the Ninth Conference on Machine Translation*, pages 118–123, Miami, Florida, USA. Association for Computational Linguistics.

Albert Q. Jiang, Alexandre Sablayrolles, Arthur Mensch, Chris Bamford, Devendra Singh Chaplot, Diego de las Casas, Florian Bressand, Gianna Lengyel, Guillaume Lample, Lucile Saulnier, Lélio Renard Lavaud, Marie-Anne Lachaux, Pierre Stock, Teven Le Scao, Thibaut Lavril, Thomas Wang, Timothée Lacroix, and William El Sayed. 2023. Mistral 7b. *Preprint*, arXiv:2310.06825.

J. Johnson, M. Douze, and H. Jegou. 2021. Billion-scale similarity search with gpus. *IEEE Transactions on Big Data*, 7(03):535–547.

Guillaume Klein, Yoon Kim, Yuntian Deng, Jean Senellart, and Alexander M Rush. 2017. OpenNMT: Open-source toolkit for neural machine translation. *Computing Research Repository*, arXiv:1701.02810.

Tom Kocmi, Eleftherios Avramidis, Rachel Bawden, Ondřej Bojar, Anton Dvorkovich, Christian Federmann, Mark Fishel, Markus Freitag, Thamme Gowda, Roman Grundkiewicz, Barry Haddow, Marzena Karpinska, Philipp Koehn, Benjamin Marie, Christof Monz, Kenton Murray, Masaaki Nagata, Martin Popel, Maja Popović, Mariya Shmatova, Steinthór Steingrímsson, and Vilém Zouhar. 2024. Findings of the WMT24 general machine translation shared task: The LLM era is here but MT is not solved yet. In *Proceedings of the Ninth Conference on Machine Translation*, pages 1–46, Miami, Florida, USA. Association for Computational Linguistics.

Tom Kocmi, Eleftherios Avramidis, Rachel Bawden, Ondřej Bojar, Anton Dvorkovich, Christian Federmann, Mark Fishel, Markus Freitag, Thamme Gowda, Roman Grundkiewicz, Barry Haddow, Philipp Koehn, Benjamin Marie, Christof Monz, Makoto Morishita, Kenton Murray, Makoto Nagata, Toshiaki Nakazawa, Martin Popel, Maja Popović, and Mariya Shmatova. 2023. Findings of the 2023 conference on machine translation (WMT23): LLMs are here but not quite there yet. In *Proceedings of the Eighth Conference on Machine Translation*, pages 1–42, Singapore. Association for Computational Linguistics.

Philipp Koehn. 2004. Statistical significance tests for machine translation evaluation. In *Proceedings of the 2004 Conference on Empirical Methods in Natural Language Processing*, pages 388–395, Barcelona, Spain. Association for Computational Linguistics.

Taku Kudo and John Richardson. 2018. SentencePiece: A simple and language independent subword tokenizer and detokenizer for neural text processing. In *Proceedings of the 2018 Conference on Empirical Methods in Natural Language Processing: System Demonstrations*, pages 66–71, Brussels, Belgium. Association for Computational Linguistics.

Yasmin Moslem, Rejwanul Haque, John D. Kelleher, and Andy Way. 2023a. Adaptive machine translation with large language models. In *Proceedings of the 24th Annual Conference of the European Association for Machine Translation*, pages 227–237, Tampere,

Finland. European Association for Machine Translation.

Yasmin Moslem, Rejwanul Haque, and Andy Way. 2023b. Fine-tuning large language models for adaptive machine translation. *ArXiv*, abs/2312.12740.

Yongyu Mu, Abudurexiti Reheman, Zhiquan Cao, Yuchun Fan, Bei Li, Yinqiao Li, Tong Xiao, Chunliang Zhang, and Jingbo Zhu. 2023. Augmenting large language model translators via translation memories. In *Findings of the Association for Computational Linguistics: ACL 2023*, pages 10287–10299, Toronto, Canada. Association for Computational Linguistics.

Matteo Pagliardini, Prakhar Gupta, and Martin Jaggi. 2018. Unsupervised learning of sentence embeddings using compositional n-gram features. In *Proceedings of the 2018 Conference of the North American Chapter of the Association for Computational Linguistics: Human Language Technologies, Volume 1 (Long Papers)*, pages 528–540, New Orleans, Louisiana, USA. Association for Computational Linguistics.

Maja Popović. 2015. chrF: character n-gram F-score for automatic MT evaluation. In *Proceedings of the Tenth Workshop on Statistical Machine Translation*, pages 392–395, Lisbon, Portugal. Association for Computational Linguistics.

Matt Post. 2018. A call for clarity in reporting BLEU scores. In *Proceedings of the Third Conference on Machine Translation: Research Papers*, pages 186–191, Belgium, Brussels. Association for Computational Linguistics.

Valeria Ramírez-Castañeda. 2020. Disadvantages in preparing and publishing scientific papers caused by the dominance of the english language in science: The case of colombian researchers in biological sciences. *PLoS ONE*, 15.

Abudurexiti Reheman, Tao Zhou, Yingfeng Luo, Di Yang, Tong Xiao, and Jingbo Zhu. 2023. Prompting neural machine translation with translation memories. In *Proceedings of the Thirty-Seventh AAAI Conference on Artificial Intelligence and Thirty-Fifth Conference on Innovative Applications of Artificial Intelligence and Thirteenth Symposium on Educational Advances in Artificial Intelligence*, AAAI'23/IAAI'23/EAAI'23. AAAI Press.

Ricardo Rei, Craig Stewart, Ana C Farinha, and Alon Lavie. 2020. COMET: A neural framework for MT evaluation. In *Proceedings of the 2020 Conference on Empirical Methods in Natural Language Processing (EMNLP)*, pages 2685–2702, Online. Association for Computational Linguistics.

Dimitrios Roussis, Vassilis Papavassiliou, Prokopis Prokopidis, Stelios Piperidis, and Vassilis Katsouros. 2022. Scipar: A collection of parallel corpora from scientific abstracts. In *International Conference on Language Resources and Evaluation*.

Dimitris Roussis, Sokratis Sofianopoulos, and Stelios Piperidis. 2024. Enhancing scientific discourse: Machine translation for the scientific domain. In *Proceedings of the 25th Annual Conference of the European Association for Machine Translation (Volume 1)*, pages 275–285, Sheffield, UK. European Association for Machine Translation (EAMT).

Javad Pourmostafa Roshan Sharami, Dimitar Shterionov, and Pieter Spronck. 2021. Selecting parallel in-domain sentences for neural machine translation using monolingual texts. *ArXiv*, abs/2112.06096.

Emma Steigerwald, Valeria Ramírez-Castañeda, Débora Y C Brandt, András Báldi, Julie Teresa Shapiro, Lynne Bowker, and Rebecca D Tarvin. 2022. Overcoming language barriers in academia: Machine translation tools and a vision for a multilingual future. *BioScience*, 72(10):988–998.

Arda Tezcan, Bram Bulté, and Bram Vanroy. 2021. Towards a better integration of fuzzy matches in neural machine translation through data augmentation. *Informatics*, 8(1).

Arda Tezcan, Alina Skidanova, and Thomas Moerman. 2024. Improving fuzzy match augmented neural machine translation in specialised domains through synthetic data. *Prague Bull. Math. Linguistics*, 122:9–42.

Bram Vanroy, Arda Tezcan, and Lieve Macken. 2023. MATEO: MAchine Translation Evaluation Online. In *Proceedings of the 24th Annual Conference of the European Association for Machine Translation*, pages 499–500. European Association for Machine Translation (EAMT).

Ashish Vaswani, Noam Shazeer, Niki Parmar, Jakob Uszkoreit, Llion Jones, Aidan N Gomez, Ł ukasz Kaiser, and Illia Polosukhin. 2017a. Attention is all you need. In *Advances in Neural Information Processing Systems*, volume 30. Curran Associates, Inc.

Ashish Vaswani, Noam Shazeer, Niki Parmar, Jakob Uszkoreit, Llion Jones, Aidan N Gomez, Łukasz Kaiser, and Illia Polosukhin. 2017b. Attention is all you need. In *Advances in neural information processing systems*, pages 5998–6008.

Aman Kassahun Wassie, Mahdi Molaei, and Yasmin Moslem. 2025. Domain-specific translation with open-source large language models: Resource-oriented analysis. *Preprint*, arXiv:2412.05862.

Jitao Xu, Josep Crego, and Jean Senellart. 2020. Boosting neural machine translation with similar translations. In *Proceedings of the 58th Annual Meeting of the Association for Computational Linguistics*, pages 1580–1590, Online. Association for Computational Linguistics.

Dataset	Avg. No. Tokens (Std. Dev.)	
	English	French
Neuroscience (train)	23.8 (11.6)	27.5 (13.2)
Neuroscience (val.)	23.7 (11.7)	27.4 (13.3)
Neuroscience (test)	23.3 (11.7)	27.3 (13.7)
Climatology (train)	25.8 (12.1)	29.2 (13.7)
Climatology (val.)	26.1 (12.3)	29.5 (13.6)
Climatology (test)	26.3 (12.8)	29.4 (14.3)
Mobility (train)	26.2 (13.1)	28.3 (13.8)
Mobility (val.)	26.5 (13.2)	28.7 (14.2)
Mobility (test)	26.3 (12.8)	28.4 (13.8)
Scipar	25.1 (13.2)	27.9 (14.4)
EuroPat	30.7 (18.6)	30.9 (18.4)
ParaCrawl	22.3 (11.7)	24.4 (12.9)

Table 5: Average number of tokens per dataset prior to sub-word tokenization, with the standard deviation shown in parentheses.

A Appendix

A.1 Dataset Statistics

A.2 Sent2vec Hyper-parameters

To train sent2vec models, we used the hyper-parameters that are suggested in the description paper (Pagliardini et al., 2018) for a sent2vec model trained on Wikipedia data containing both unigrams and bigrams. The hyper-parameters values are provided in Table 6.

Hyper-parameter	Value
embedding dimension	480
minimum word count	8
minimum target word count	20
initial learning rate	0.2
epochs	9
sub-sampling hyper-parameter	5×10^{-6}
bigrams dropped per sentence	4
number of negatives sampled	10

Table 6: Hyper-parameters for training sent2vec models.

A.3 FAISS Configuration

For efficient retrieval of FMs, we created a flat FAISS index with an inverted file system (IVF) of 4096 clusters. We used cosine similarity as the match metric by adding the L2-normalized vectors of the sentence representation to the index and using an L2-normalized sentence vector as an input query. For more information on FAISS, please see `https://github.com/facebookresearch/faiss/wiki`.

A.4 NMT Training Data and Vocabulary Sizes

System	Neuroscience	Climatology	Mobility
1d	98,857	95,694	106,282
3d	300,833	300,833	300,833
3d_FM	601,666	601,666	601,666
3d+Ext	22,161,961	22,161,961	22,161,961
3d+Ext_FM	44,323,799	44,323,799	44,323,799
3d+ExtTF	5,358,062	10,486,732	9,125,589
3d+ExtTF_FM	10,708,321	20,969,963	18,249,664

Table 7: The total number of bilingual sentence pairs used for training the NMT systems, per discipline.

System	Lang.	Neurosci.	Climat.	Mobility
1d	src	22,216	25,049	27,101
	tgt	21,414	24,448	25,814
3d	src	32,791	32,791	32,791
	tgt	32,274	32,274	32,274
3d_FM	src	35,936	35,936	35,936
	trg	32,274	32,274	32,274
3d+Ext	src	67,995	67,995	67,995
	tgt	62,333	62,333	62,333
3d+Ext_FM	src	69,031	69,031	69,031
	tgt	62,333	62,333	62,333
3d+ExtTF	src	55,516	57,280	63,512
	tgt	51,869	53,669	58,643
3d+ExtTF_FM	src	56,506	58,314	64,248
	tgt	51,869	53,669	58,643

Table 8: Vocabulary sizes (source/target) of the NMT systems, per discipline.

A.5 NMT Hyper-parameters

Hyper-parameter	Value
source/target embedding dimension	512
size of hidden layers	512
feed-forward layers	2048
number of heads	8
number of layers	6
batch size	32
gradient accumulation	4
dropout	0.1
warm-up steps	8000
optimizer	Adam

Table 9: Common hyper-parameter values used for training the NMT systems.

We performed evaluations on a given validation set after every 10% of the training data was processed during each NMT training (i.e. 10 evaluations per epoch).

A.6 LLM Prompts

The zero-shot and in-context learning (i.e. few-shot) experiments employed different prompt templates depending on the model type. Table 10 presents the prompt templates used for the Mistral-7B-v0.3 base model, following Moslem et al. (2023a), and for all the instruct models, following Format 1 described in Alves et al. (2023).

Model	Translation Type	Prompt Template
Base	Zero-shot	English: ⟨source_segment⟩ French:
Base	Few-shot (e.g., 2-shot)	English: ⟨source_fuzzy_match$_2$⟩ French: ⟨target_fuzzy_match$_2$⟩ English: ⟨source_fuzzy_match$_1$⟩ French: ⟨target_fuzzy_match$_1$⟩ English: ⟨source_segment⟩ French:
Instruct	Zero-shot	Translate the source text from X to Y. Source: ⟨source_segment⟩ Target:
Instruct	Few-shot (e.g., 2-shot)	Translate the source text from X to Y. Source: ⟨source_fuzzy_match$_2$⟩ Target: ⟨target_fuzzy_match$_2$⟩ Translate the source text from X to Y. Source: ⟨source_fuzzy_match$_1$⟩ Target: ⟨target_fuzzy_match$_1$⟩ Translate the source text from X to Y. Source: ⟨source_segment⟩ Target:

Table 10: Prompt templates used for zero-shot and few-shot translation with the different LLMs tested in this study. In the few-shot templates, fuzzy matches are ordered from the nth-most similar match to the most similar (where n refers to the number of shots), followed by the source segment to be translated.

Author Index

Association for Computational Linguistics
209 N. Eighth Street
Stroudsburg, Pennsylvania 18360

ISBN 979-8-3313-2673-9

CURRAN ASSOCIATES INC.
proceedings.com